Adobe® Dreamweaver® CS4

Level 2

Adobe® Dreamweaver® CS4: Level 2

Part Number: 084054
Course Edition: 1.0

NOTICES

DISCLAIMER: While Element K Corporation takes care to ensure the accuracy and quality of these materials, we cannot guarantee their accuracy, and all materials are provided without any warranty whatsoever, including, but not limited to, the implied warranties of merchantability or fitness for a particular purpose. The name used in the data files for this course is that of a fictitious company. Any resemblance to current or future companies is purely coincidental. We do not believe we have used anyone's name in creating this course, but if we have, please notify us and we will change the name in the next revision of the course. Element K is an independent provider of integrated training solutions for individuals, businesses, educational institutions, and government agencies. Use of screenshots, photographs of another entity's products, or another entity's product name or service in this book is for editorial purposes only. No such use should be construed to imply sponsorship or endorsement of the book by, nor any affiliation of such entity with Element K. This courseware may contain links to sites on the Internet that are owned and operated by third parties (the "External Sites"). Element K is not responsible for the availability of, or the content located on or through, any External Site. Please contact Element K if you have any concerns regarding such links or External Sites.

TRADEMARK NOTICES Element K and the Element K logo are trademarks of Element K Corporation and its affiliates.

Adobe® Dreamweaver® CS4 and Adobe® Photoshop® CS4 are registered trademarks of Adobe Systems Incorporated in the U.S. and other countries; the Adobe Systems products and services discussed or described may be trademarks of Adobe Systems Incorporated. All other product names and services used throughout this course may be common law or registered trademarks of their respective proprietors.

Copyright © 2009 Element K Corporation. All rights reserved. Screenshots used for illustrative purposes are the property of the software proprietor. This publication, or any part thereof, may not be reproduced or transmitted in any form or by any means, electronic or mechanical, including photocopying, recording, storage in an information retrieval system, or otherwise, without express written permission of Element K, 500 Canal View Boulevard, Rochester, NY 14623, (585) 240-7500, (800) 478-7788. Element K Courseware's World Wide Web site is located at www.elementkcourseware.com.

This book conveys no rights in the software or other products about which it was written; all use or licensing of such software or other products is the responsibility of the user according to terms and conditions of the owner. Do not make illegal copies of books or software. If you believe that this book, related materials, or any other Element K materials are being reproduced or transmitted without permission, please call (800) 478-7788.

HELP US IMPROVE OUR COURSEWARE

Your comments are important to us. Please contact us at Element K Press LLC, 1-800-478-7788, 500 Canal View Boulevard, Rochester, NY 14623, Attention: Product Planning, or through our Web site at http://support.elementkcourseware.com.

Adobe® Dreamweaver® CS4: Level 2

Lesson 1: Working in Code View
    A. Use Coding Tools 2
    B. Search for and Replace Code 11
    C. Add Design Notes and Comments 18

Lesson 2: Formatting with Advanced CSS Techniques
    A. Use External Style Sheets 28
    B. Create a Layout Using CSS 39
    C. Apply Rollover Effects Using CSS 55

Lesson 3: Working with AP Elements
    A. Create AP Elements 62
    B. Control AP Elements 73

Lesson 4: Working with Spry Elements
    A. Use Spry Interface Widgets 86
    B. Modify Spry Widgets 98
    C. Use Spry Data Sets 101

Lesson 5: Creating a Form
    A. Set Up a Form 116
    B. Add Form Elements 121
    C. Validate a Form 131

Lesson 6: Integrating External Files with Dreamweaver
    A. Integrate Photoshop Images in Dreamweaver 144

B. Insert Media Objects **151**
　　　C. Integrate XML-Based Data **157**

Appendix A: Working with Adobe Bridge and Adobe Device Central
　　　A. Explore Adobe Bridge **168**
　　　B. Apply Metadata and Keywords to Assets in Adobe Bridge **175**
　　　C. Work with Stacks and Filters in Adobe Bridge **180**
　　　D. Preview Web Pages in Device Central **183**

Appendix B: New Features in Adobe Dreamweaver CS4

Lesson Labs **189**

Solutions **201**

Glossary **203**

Index **205**

About This Course

You created basic web pages. You may now need to develop websites with advanced functionality. In this course, you will use the advanced features of Adobe® Dreamweaver® CS4 to design and develop professional-looking websites.

Though you can develop a website with pages containing only images and text, there may be times when you need to enhance the presentation of content on your website and provide more useful functions. By using the advanced features of Adobe® Dreamweaver® CS4, you can develop professional-looking web pages that will attract site visitors.

Course Description

Target Student

This course is intended for web designers, developers, graphic artists, media marketing personnel, and anyone who needs to utilize Adobe® Dreamweaver® CS4 to create or enhance websites using advanced techniques.

Course Prerequisites

To ensure your success in this course, it is recommended that you first take the following Element K courses, *Adobe® Dreamweaver® CS4: Level 1* and *Cascading Style Sheets (Second Edition): Level 1* or have equivalent knowledge.

How to Use This Book

As a Learning Guide

Each lesson covers one broad topic or set of related topics. Lessons are arranged in order of increasing proficiency with *Adobe® Dreamweaver® CS4*; skills you acquire in one lesson are used and developed in subsequent lessons. For this reason, you should work through the lessons in sequence.

Each lesson is organized into results-oriented topics. Topics include all the relevant and supporting information you need to master *Adobe® Dreamweaver® CS4*, and activities allow you to apply this information to practical hands-on examples.

You get to try out each new skill on a specially prepared sample file. This saves you typing time and allows you to concentrate on the skill at hand. Through the use of sample files, hands-on activities, illustrations that give you feedback at crucial steps, and supporting background information, this book provides you with the foundation and structure to learn *Adobe® Dreamweaver® CS4* quickly and easily.

As a Review Tool

Any method of instruction is only as effective as the time and effort you are willing to invest in it. In addition, some of the information that you learn in class may not be important to you immediately, but it may become important later on. For this reason, we encourage you to spend some time reviewing the topics and activities after the course. For additional challenge when reviewing activities, try the "What You Do" column before looking at the "How You Do It" column.

As a Reference

The organization and layout of the book make it easy to use as a learning tool and as an after-class reference. You can use this book as a first source for definitions of terms, background information on given topics, and summaries of procedures.

Course Icons

Icon	Description
	A **Caution Note** makes students aware of potential negative consequences of an action, setting, or decision that are not easily known.
	Display Slide provides a prompt to the instructor to display a specific slide. Display Slides are included in the Instructor Guide only.
	An **Instructor Note** is a comment to the instructor regarding delivery, classroom strategy, classroom tools, exceptions, and other special considerations. Instructor Notes are included in the Instructor Guide only.
	Notes Page indicates a page that has been left intentionally blank for students to write on.
	A **Student Note** provides additional information, guidance, or hints about a topic or task.
	A **Version Note** indicates information necessary for a specific version of software.

Course Objectives

In this course, you will develop professional-looking web pages using the Adobe® Dreamweaver® CS4 application.

You will:

- work in Code view and use coding tools and features available in Dreamweaver.
- format web pages using advanced CSS techniques.
- work with AP elements.
- work with Spry elements.
- create and validate forms.
- integrate external files with Dreamweaver.
- work with Adobe® Bridge® and Adobe® Device Central® applications.

Course Requirements

Hardware

- Intel® Pentium® IV processor
- 512 MB of RAM
- 1 GB of available disk space for software installation, and an additional 10 MB for the course data files
- 256-color monitor capable of 1024 x 768 resolution
- DVD-ROM drive
- Internet connection

Software

- Adobe® Dreamweaver® CS4
- Microsoft® Internet Explorer® 6.0
- Adobe® Photoshop® CS4
- Adobe® Flash® Player 9 or above for Mozilla® Firefox®
- Shockwave® Player

Class Setup

1. Install Windows XP Professional on the C drive using the following parameters:
    a. Accept the license agreement.
    b. Create a 4 GB partition on the C drive.
    c. Format the C partition to NTFS.
    d. Select the appropriate regional and language settings.
    e. Enter the appropriate name and organization for your environment.
    f. Enter the product key.
    g. For each student computer, configure the settings:

- Name of computer: **Computer#** (where # is a unique integer representing the student computer).
- Administrator password: *password.*
- Select your time zone.
- Select the **Typical** network configuration.

2. Install Adobe® Dreamweaver® CS4. If you already have a full version of Adobe® Dreamweaver® CS4 installed on your computer, this course will run best if you uninstall and reinstall Dreamweaver to reset the application to the default settings. *Warning:* Uninstalling and reinstalling Dreamweaver will require you to re-enter the serial number of the program. If you do not have the serial number and installation CD available, do not uninstall.

   If you are unable to uninstall or reinstall the program, you should remove the Our Global Company site, if it exists. Launch Dreamweaver and choose **Site→Manage Sites.** In the **Manage Sites** dialog box, click the Our Global company site, if it is listed, and click **Remove.** Exit Dreamweaver.

3. Make sure that you have web browser software properly installed on your computer. It is preferable to have both Microsoft® Internet Explorer® and Mozilla® Firefox® installed, since they are the two most popular browsers.

4. Set up Internet Explorer to allow ActiveX controls.
   a. Open Internet Explorer.
   b. Choose **Tools→Internet Options.**
   c. In the **Internet Options** dialog box, select the **Advanced** tab.
   d. In the **Settings** list box, in the **Security** section, check the **Allow active content to run in files on My Computer** check box.
   e. Click **Apply** and click **OK.**

5. Make sure that file extensions are enabled.
   a. Open **My Computer.**
   b. Choose **Tools→Folder Options.** The **Folder Options** dialog box appears.
   c. Select the **View** tab, uncheck the **Hide extensions for known file types** check box, and click **OK.**

6. Install Adobe® Photoshop® CS4 Professional, accepting all default settings.

7. Download and install the Flash plug-in for the Firefox browser. After installing the plug-in you will have to restart the computer for the installation to be complete.

8. The last activity in Lesson 5, "Testing Forms," requires configuration of Microsoft® Outlook® Express or any mail client on your computer.

9. On the course CD-ROM, run the 084054dd.exe self-extracting file located within. This will install a folder named 084054Data on your C drive. This folder contains all the data files that you will use to complete this course.

10. In addition to the specific setup procedures needed for this class to run properly, you should also check the Element K Press product support website at **http://support.elementkcourseware.com** for more information. Any updates about this course will be posted there.

List of Additional Files

Printed with each activity is a list of files students open to complete that activity. Many activities also require additional files that students do not open, but are needed to support the file(s) students are working with. These supporting files are included with the student data files on the course CD-ROM or data disk. Do not delete these files.

1 Working in Code View

Lesson Time: 1 hour(s), 5 minutes

Lesson Objectives:

In this lesson, you will work in Code view and use coding tools and features available in Dreamweaver.

You will:

- Use coding tools.
- Search for and replace code.
- Add design notes and comments.

Introduction

You created web pages using Adobe® Dreamweaver®. During the course of your work, you will often need to work directly with code. In this lesson, you will work in Code view.

Although Dreamweaver largely eliminates the need to work with code, there may be times when modifications to web pages in Design view are difficult to make. Using various coding tools and features available in Dreamweaver, you can simplify coding tasks even when the pages contain extensive code.

TOPIC A
Use Coding Tools

You used Design view of Dreamweaver to build web pages. You may now need to familiarize yourself with working in Code view. In this topic, you will use coding tools and features available in Dreamweaver.

While designing web pages, controlling the appearance of page elements in Design view may sometimes not provide the intended output. As a web developer, you may often want to directly work with code to modify it. Using coding tools and features available in Dreamweaver will help you accomplish this with ease.

Coding Features

Dreamweaver provides various coding features that help you edit code. The following table describes coding features.

Feature	Description
Code hints	Lists the available tags when you type the opening angular bracket (<) and the available attributes when you type a tag name. These hints also allow you to insert the required item into code.
CODE INSPECTOR panel	Displays code in a separate panel and allows you to work with it.
Code Navigation	Lists the JavaScript™ or VBScript functions that you have used in code, and allows you to navigate to the required function.
Coding context menu	Lists the most frequently used coding tools, such as **Code Hint Tools, Insert Tag, Collapse Selection, Find and Replace,** and **Reference,** on a contextual menu when you right-click in Code view.
Quick Tag Editor	Allows you to edit existing tags and their attributes, or insert new tags.
Tag Editor dialog box	Displays the current values of the attributes of the selected tag and allows you to modify the attributes.
Tag Chooser dialog box	Allows you to insert tags by selecting a tag from the tag library.
TAG INSPECTOR panel	Allows you to edit or add attributes to the selected tag.

The REFERENCE Panel

The **REFERENCE** panel in the **Results** panel group displays detailed descriptions of tags and their uses and attributes. It can be used to refer to accessibility standards and information on tags, objects, and CSS properties that can be applied in Dreamweaver and related to different coding and markup languages such as HTML, CSS, JavaScript, XML. The O'REILLY HTML Reference is the most commonly used reference material for HTML tags.

The Coding Toolbar

The *Coding toolbar* is displayed when you work either in Code view or in the **CODE INSPECTOR** panel. The toolbar contains options that help you perform different coding operations.

The table describes the options available on the **Coding** toolbar.

Option	Description
Open Documents	Lists the documents that are open and allows you to switch between them.
Show Code Navigator	Displays the Code Navigator for the current selection or current insertion point.
Collapse Full Tag	Collapses the content within the opening and closing tags.
Collapse Selection	Collapses code within the selection.
Expand All	Expands collapsed code.
Select Parent Tag	Selects the opening and closing tags and the content that surrounds the insertion point. You can select the outermost tags by clicking this button repeatedly.
Balance Braces	Selects content within parentheses, braces, or square brackets. You can select the outermost braces by clicking this button repeatedly.
Line Numbers	Shows or hides line numbers for code.
Highlight Invalid Code	Highlights invalid code in yellow.
Syntax Error Alerts in Info Bar	Displays syntax errors on an information bar at the top of the document window.
Apply Comment	Applies comments to the selected code or text, or inserts new comment tags if no code or text is selected.
Remove Comment	Removes the comment tags from the selected code or text.
Wrap Tag	Wraps the selected code with the tag you specify.
Recent Snippets	Lists recently used snippets and allows you to add one of them to code. This option also allows you to display the **SNIPPETS** panel.
Move or Convert CSS	Allows you to convert inline CSS to CSS rules or move CSS rules to another location.
Indent Code	Moves the selected code to the right.

Option	Description
Outdent Code	Moves the selected code to the left.
Format Source Code	Applies pre-specified formatting to the selected code or to the entire web page if no code is selected. You can modify the settings that help format code by selecting the **Code Format Settings** option and then editing the tag libraries using the **Edit Tag Libraries** option.

Code Hints

When you type in Code view, the code hints feature displays a contextual menu that allows you to choose code and insert it into your document. This menu displays the available tags, attributes, and parameters that can be inserted at the current insertion point in the document. You can use code hint tools to specify the values for colors, URLs, and fonts. Code hints are available for various coding languages and technologies, such as HTML, CSS, JavaScript, ColdFusion, and Ajax.

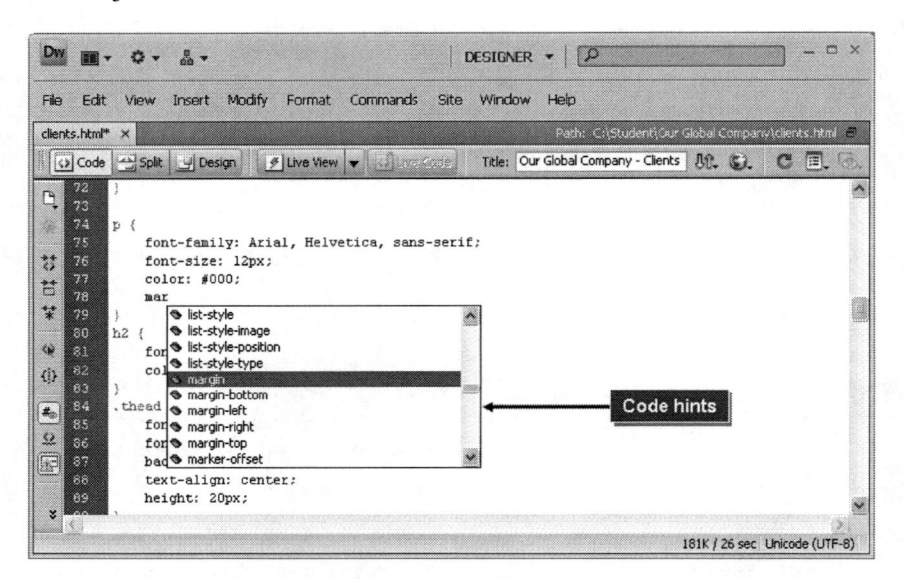

Figure 1-1: Code hints displaying CSS properties.

How to Use Coding Tools

Procedure Reference: Use Coding Features

To use coding features:

1. Open a web page.
2. Display the selected web page in Code view.
   - Choose **View→Code.**
   - Or, on the **Document** toolbar, click **Code.**
3. In Code view, position the insertion point at a location to add code.
4. Add tags and attributes.
   - Type tags and attributes.
   - Use the code hints feature to insert tags, attributes, and values.
     a. Type < and from the drop-down list, select a tag and press **Enter.**
     b. If necessary, add attributes and their values using the code hints feature.
     c. Type > to close the tag.
   - Or, use the **Tag Chooser** dialog box to insert tags and attributes.
     a. Display the **Tag Chooser** dialog box.
        - Right-click and choose **Insert Tag.**
        - Or, choose **Insert→Tag.**
     b. In the top pane, in the list box displayed on the left, expand a sub-tree, and select a category to display the tags in the list box displayed on the right.
     c. In the list box displayed on the right, select a tag and click **Insert** to insert it in the document.
     d. In the **Tag Editor - <tag>** dialog box, set attributes and click **OK.**
5. If necessary, in Code view, position the insertion point at a location to add or modify attributes and their values.
6. If necessary, modify or set attributes for a tag.
   - Set values using the **Tag Editor** dialog box.
     a. Display the **Tag Editor** dialog box.
        - Right-click the tag and choose **Edit Tag <tag name>.**
        - Or, choose **Modify→Edit Tag.**
     b. Select a category and edit its attributes.
     c. Click **OK** to apply settings.
   - Or, set values using the **TAG INSPECTOR** panel.
     a. Choose **Window→Tag Inspector.**
     b. If necessary, click **Attributes.**
     c. In the text boxes to the right of attribute names, specify values for attributes.

7. If necessary, inspect code using the **CODE INSPECTOR** panel.
    a. Choose **Window→Code Inspector.**
    b. In the **CODE INSPECTOR** panel, on the toolbar at the top, click a button to perform an action.
    c. In the **CODE INSPECTOR** panel, on the **Coding** toolbar, click a button to perform an operation.
    d. Close the **CODE INSPECTOR** panel.

Procedure Reference: Use the Coding Toolbar

To use the **Coding** toolbar:
1. Display the web page in Code view.
2. If necessary, choose **View→Toolbars→Coding** to view the **Coding** toolbar.
3. On the **Coding** toolbar, click a button to perform an operation.

Procedure Reference: Refer to a Tag Using the REFERENCE Panel

To refer to a tag using the **REFERENCE** panel:
1. Display the web page in Code view.
2. Display the description of the tag in the **REFERENCE** panel.
   - Right-click a tag and choose **Reference.**
   - Or, access the **REFERENCE** panel to view the description.
      a. Choose **Window→Results→Reference** to display the **REFERENCE** panel.
      b. If necessary, from the **Book** drop-down list, select the required reference material.
      c. From the **Tag** drop-down list, select a tag.

Adobe® Dreamweaver® CS4: Level 2

ACTIVITY 1-1
Inserting Code

Data Files:

ourcompany.html

Before You Begin:
1. Open the Dreamweaver application.
2. In the **Site Definition** wizard, using the **Basic** tab, define the Our Global Company site using the data from the C:\084054Data\Our Global Company folder.

Scenario:
You want to enhance the formatting of the Our Company page. You decide to present information in the "Areas of expertise" section as a list of items. You also want to ensure that code for the page is formatted properly.

What You Do	How You Do It
1. Format the "Areas of expertise" section.	a. In the **FILES** panel, scroll down and double-click **ourcompany.html** to open the file.
	b. On the **Document** toolbar, click **Design** to switch to Design view.
	c. In the document window, in the second paragraph, click at the beginning of the text "Change management", hold down **Shift,** and click at the end of the text "Employee and customer attitude research" to select it.
	d. In the **Property Inspector,** click the **Unordered List** button.
	e. Observe that the list is not formatted properly.

- Our areas of expertise include:
  Change management
  Performance management
  Strategic planning
  Business process reengineering
  HR Systems development and implementation
  Employee and customer attitude research

Lesson 1: Working in Code View 7

2.	Modify the unordered list.	a.	On the **Document** toolbar, click **Code** to switch to Code view.
		b.	In the line numbers section, click **154** and press **Delete** to delete the `<ul>` tag.
		c.	In line 154, click before the `<li>` tag, hold down **Shift,** click after the `<li>` tag to select it, and press **Delete.**
		d.	In line 155, click before the text "Change management", and type **<**
		e.	Observe that the code hints appear.
		f.	Type **u**
		g.	In the code hints, verify that **<>ul** is selected, press **Enter,** and type **>**
3.	Add <li> tags for list items.	a.	Press **Enter** and type **<li>**
		b.	In line 156, click after the text "Change management", and type **</**
		c.	Observe that the `</li>` closing tag is automatically inserted by Dreamweaver.
		d.	In line 156, select the ` ` tag and delete it.
		e.	Similarly, in lines 157, 158, 159, and 160, add `<li>` and `</li>` tags and delete the ` ` tag. At the beginning of line 161, add the `<li>` tag.
		f.	Switch to Design view.
		g.	Observe that the list is formatted.

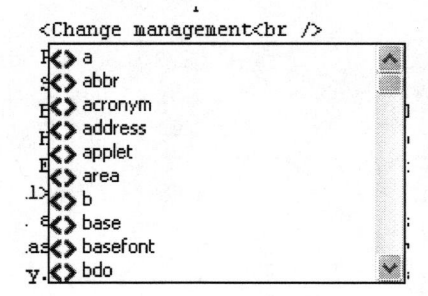

4. Indent the tags.

    a. Switch to Code view.

    b. Observe that in lines 156 through 162, the `<li>` and `</ul>` tags are not indented properly.

    c. In the line numbers section, click **156,** hold down **Shift,** and click **162.**

    d. On the **Coding** toolbar, click the **Indent Code** button, to indent the code in line numbers 156 to 162.

    e. Switch to Design view.

5. Add a header tag.

    a. Observe that the introduction sentence for the list is formatted as normal text.

    b. Choose **Window→Code Inspector** to display the **CODE INSPECTOR** panel.

    c. In the **CODE INSPECTOR** panel, in line 154, observe that tags are not applied to text.

    d. In the **CODE INSPECTOR** panel, in line 154, click at the beginning of the text "Our areas" and type **`<h4>`**

    e. In line 154, click after the text "expertise include:" and type `</` to complete the `</h4>` tag.

    f. In line 154, hold down **Shift,** click after the `<br />` tag to select it, and press **Delete.**

    g. Close the **CODE INSPECTOR** panel.

    h. Observe that the introduction sentence for the list is formatted as a sub-heading.

6. Navigate to the CSS rules.

    a. In the document window, below the first paragraph, click at the beginning of the text "Our areas of expertise include:".

    b. Observe that the Code Navigator indicator, appears.

> The Code Navigator indicator will appear a few seconds after you click in the document window.

Lesson 1: Working in Code View   9

		c.	Click the Code Navigator indicator, and in the Code Navigator, click **h4.**
		d.	Observe that the CSS rule for the `<h4>` tag is displayed in the code section of Split view.
		e.	In the line numbers section, click **79,** hold down **Shift,** and click **82.**
		f.	On the **Coding** toolbar, click the **Collapse Selection** button, to collapse the CSS rule for the `<h4>` tag.
		g.	Similarly, collapse the CSS rule for the `<h2>` tag.
7.	Add a style for the unordered list.	a.	Click at the end of line 83 and press **Enter.**
		b.	Type **ul {** and press **Enter.**
		c.	Type **li** and from the code hints, choose **list-style-type** and press **Enter.**
		d.	In the code hints, scroll down and double-click **square.**
		e.	Type **;** and press **Enter.**
		f.	Type **}** to close the CSS rule.
		g.	Save the file.
8.	Preview the page in a browser.	a.	Preview the page in Internet Explorer.
		b.	Observe that the areas of the expertise section is formatted as a list.
		c.	Close the Internet Explorer window.

TOPIC B
Search for and Replace Code

You used coding features and tools available in Dreamweaver to work with code on a web page. You may now want to quickly locate and change specific code. In this topic, you will use the **Find and Replace** command.

As the volume of code increases, locating a particular tag or piece of text in Code view can become a tedious task. By using the advanced search facilities that Dreamweaver provides, you can search for and replace code quickly and efficiently.

The Find and Replace Dialog Box

The **Find and Replace** dialog box helps you search for text, tags, and attributes of tags within code, and replace them with specified values. Using this dialog box, a search can be performed on selected text, the entire current document, a set of documents, or the entire current local site. You can also save and load search queries.

The **Find and Replace** dialog box provides four options that help perform searches on a web page.

Option	Description
Source Code	Searches for the specified text in code. The text can be a tag or content displayed within a tag.
Text	Ignores HTML tags and searches for the specified text on the web page.
Text (Advanced)	Searches for the specified text in code. Advanced searches can be performed for text that is inside or not inside a tag, with or without specific attributes, and containing or not containing text or specific tags.
Specific Tag	Searches for the specified tag in code. Advanced searches can be performed for tags that are inside or not inside another tag, with or without specific attributes, and containing or not containing text or specific tags. Various actions, such as replacing or removing the tag and its content, setting or removing attributes of the tag, and adding content before or after the start or end tags, can be performed on the tags that match the search criteria.

Saving Queries

You can save the queries that you specify in the **Find and Replace** dialog box for later use. Saving queries is helpful if you use the same search conditions frequently. It will also be useful if you need to specify multiple conditions in the **Find and Replace** dialog box. By saving queries, you can save time, and avoid having to specify the search conditions each time. You can also load the saved queries and use them in other documents.

The SEARCH Panel

The **SEARCH** panel in the **Results** panel group displays the search results for a query specified in the **Find and Replace** dialog box. It lists the file name and each occurrence of the specified text or code. You can navigate to a particular occurrence of the search result by double-clicking it. This panel also allows you to display the **Find and Replace** dialog box and save the search results as a report in an XML format.

Regular Expressions

Regular expressions are patterns that are used to match characters in text. You can use regular expressions in searches when you need to match characters that are not known.

Special Character	*Matches*
^	Characters that start with the search text.
$	Characters that end with the search text.
*	Character combinations with zero or more occurrences of the preceding character in the search text.
+	Character combinations with one or more occurrences of the preceding character in the search text.
?	Character combinations with at most one occurrence of the preceding character in the search text.
a|b	Either the search text *a* or the search text *b*.
[abc]	Character *a, b,* or *c*. Any number of characters can be enclosed within the brackets and one of them will be matched. For a range of characters, specify them with a hyphen. For example, specifying [s-v] will include searches for the characters s, t, u, and v.
[^abc]	Any character other than *a, b,* or *c*. Any number of characters can be enclosed within the brackets. To exclude a range of characters, specify them with a hyphen.
\d	Any digit from 0 to 9.
\D	Any character other than a digit.
\w	Any alphanumeric character.

How to Search for and Replace Code

Procedure Reference: Search for and Replace Code

To search for and replace code:

1. Display the required web page in Code view.
2. Display the **Find and Replace** dialog box.
   - Choose **Edit→Find and Replace.**
   - Or, in the **Results** panel group, in the **SEARCH** panel, click the **Find and Replace** button.
3. From the **Find in** drop-down list, select an option to specify the location to be searched.
4. From the **Search** drop-down list, select an option.
5. Specify the item to be searched for.
   - In the **Find** text box, type the code to be searched for.
   - From the drop-down list to the right of the **Search** drop-down list, select the tag to be searched for.

   > The **Find** text box is not visible when the **Specific Tag** option is selected in the **Search** drop-down list.

6. If necessary, specify the settings for the advanced search.
   a. From the drop-down list to the right of the Minus button (**-**), select an option.
   b. From the second drop-down list to the right of the Minus button (**-**), select the required tag or attribute.
   c. From the third drop-down list to the right of the Minus button (**-**), select an option.
   d. In the text box to the right of the third drop-down list, type the value to be searched.
7. If necessary, click the Plus button (**+**) to specify additional parameters for the search.
8. If necessary, click the Minus button (**-**) to remove the specified parameter.
9. If necessary, specify the actions to be performed when the search item is found.
   - In the **Replace** text box, type the new content.
   - From the **Action** drop-down list, select the required action to be performed and then specify values.

   > The **Replace** text box is not visible when the **Specific Tag** option is selected in the **Search** drop-down list; the **Action** drop-down list is displayed in its place.

10. If necessary, in the **Options** section, specify the appropriate options.
11. Click **Find Next** to find the search pattern.
12. If necessary, click **Find All** to display all the occurrences of the search pattern in the **SEARCH** panel of the **Results** panel group.
13. If necessary, click **Replace** to replace the found search pattern with the specified value.

14. If necessary, click **Replace All** to replace all the occurrences of the search pattern with the value specified in the **Replace** text box.

Additional Search Options

The **Options** section in the **Find and Replace** dialog box provides additional search options.

- The **Match case** option restricts the search for text that matches the casing of text specified in the **Find** text box.
- The **Ignore whitespace** option allows ignoring multiple spaces while searching for text in the document.
- The **Match whole word** option locates only whole words that match the text specified in the **Find** text box.
- The **Use regular expression** option allows the search for specific patterns using a regular expression.

ACTIVITY 1-2
Searching for and Replacing Code

Data Files:

ourcompany.html

Before You Begin:

The ourcompany.html file is open.

Scenario:

You need to change the alternate text of the header image used on the site's pages. You want to simultaneously change the "alt" property on all pages of the site. You also want to be able to quickly find code at a later time when more pages are added to the site.

What You Do	How You Do It
1. Specify the search criteria.	a. In the document window, click the header image to select it. b. In the **Property Inspector,** observe that the **Alt** attribute is assigned the value "Our Global Company." c. Choose **Edit→Find and Replace.** d. In the **Find and Replace** dialog box, from the **Find in** drop-down list, select **Entire Current Local Site.** e. From the **Search** drop-down list, select **Specific Tag.** f. In the drop-down list to the right of the **Search** drop-down list, scroll down and select **img.** g. In the drop-down list to the right of the Minus button (-), verify that **With Attribute** is selected. h. In the second drop-down list to the right of the Minus button (-), scroll down and select **width.** i. In the third drop-down list to the right of the Minus button (-), verify that **=** is selected. j. In the last text box to the right of the Minus button (-), click and type *800*
2. Set the replacement action for the `alt` attribute.	a. In the **Action** drop-down list, verify that **Set Attribute** is selected. b. From the drop-down list to the right of the **Action** drop-down list, select **alt.** c. In the **To** text box, click and type *Our Global Company Header*

3.	Save the search query.	a.	In the **Find and Replace** dialog box, click the **Save Query** button.
		b.	If necessary, in the **Save Query** dialog box, navigate to the C:\084054Data\Our Global Company folder.
		c.	In the **Save Query** dialog box, in the **File name** text box, type *image_alttext*
		d.	Click **Save** to save the search query.
4.	Replace the alternate text on all the pages of the site.	a.	In the **Find and Replace** dialog box, click **Replace All** to replace the attribute value in all occurrences matching the specified search criteria in all the files of the site.
		b.	In the **Dreamweaver** message box, click **Yes** to modify the value of the alternate text in all instances.
		c.	In the **Replacement Errors** message box, observe the message stating that the replacement was not performed in the upcomingevents.html file, because it is based on a template with non-editable regions, and click **OK.**
		d.	In the **SEARCH** panel, observe that the results of the search are displayed.
		e.	From the **SEARCH** panel options menu, choose **Close Tab Group** to close the **Results** panel group.
		f.	Save the file.
5.	Preview the web page in a browser.	a.	Preview the page in Internet Explorer.
		b.	In the Internet Explorer window, position the mouse pointer over the header image and observe that a tooltip appears with the text "Our Global Company Header".
		c.	Close the Internet Explorer window.
		d.	Close the ourcompany.html file.

TOPIC C
Add Design Notes and Comments

You searched for pieces of code on a web page and replaced them. To keep track of changes during development, you may need to add descriptions to the web page. In this topic, you will add design notes and comments to a web page.

While developing a web page, you frequently need to write down information such as the source of images to be used or the external links to be inserted. At times, you may even need to write down creative ideas so that you can use them later to complete the web page. Using design notes and comments will help you achieve this.

Design Notes

Definition:

Design notes are notes associated with web pages. They allow you to store additional information, such as the status of a file, the assets used, and the elements to be added or modified. You can assign a name to a design note entry and specify the date on which you added the note to keep track of it. The design notes for each web page are saved in separate files in the _notes folder, in the same location where the web pages are saved.

Example:

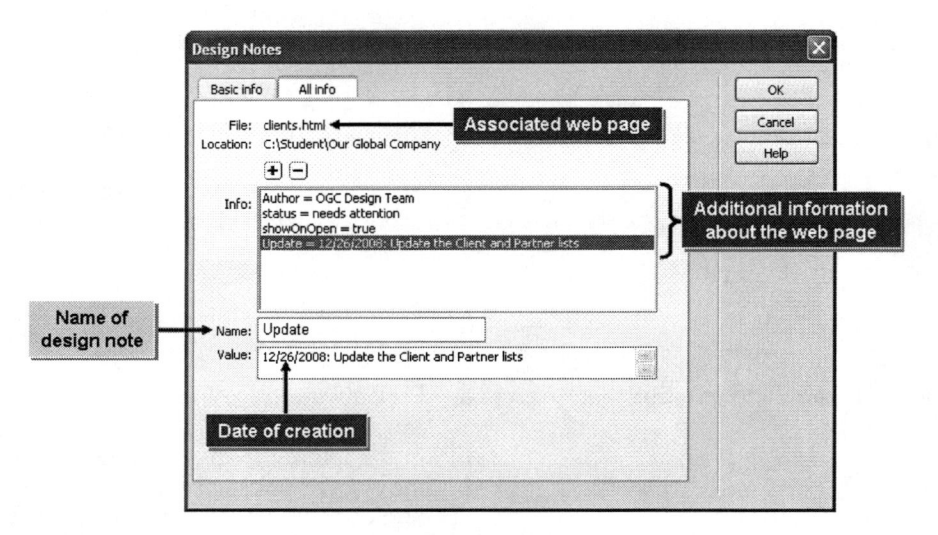

Figure 1-2: Design notes displayed for a web page.

Comments

Definition:
Comments are nonexecutable statements that describe code. Comments are placed within comment tags and can be added anywhere within code. They will not appear on the web page when viewed in a browser. Comments are commonly used by developers to explain the purpose of code, how it works, and the results of executing it.

Example:

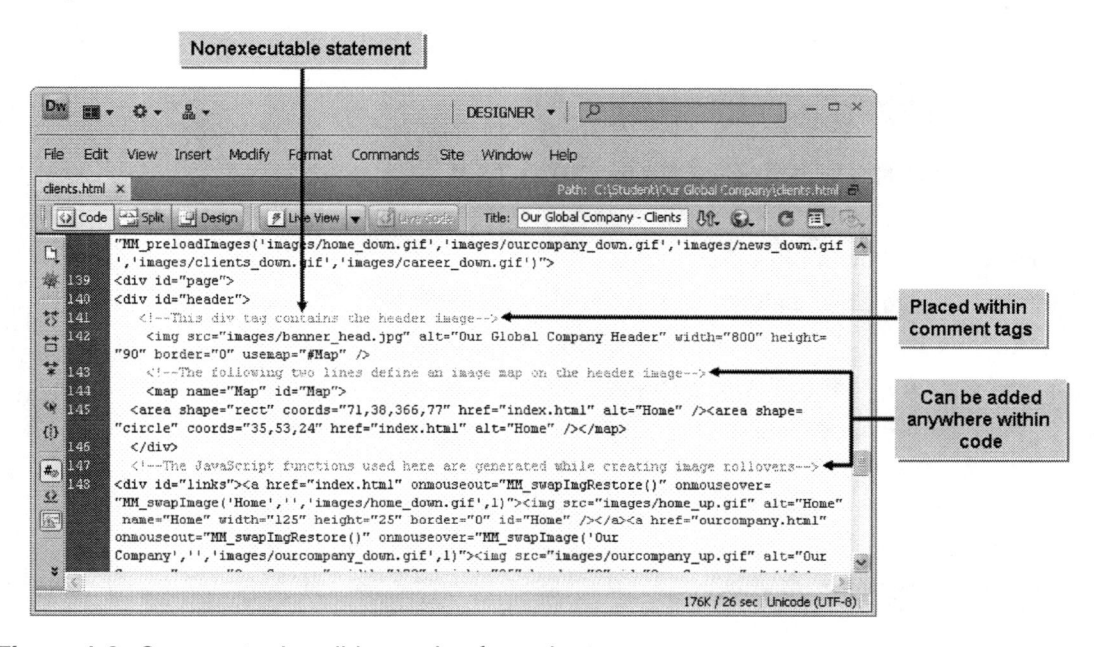

Figure 1-3: Comments describing code of a web page.

How to Add Design Notes and Comments

Procedure Reference: Insert a Comment

To insert a comment:
1. Display the web page in Code view.
2. Determine the position of the comment.
    - Select the section of code that is to be commented.
    - Click in the position where the comment is to be inserted.
3. Insert a comment.
    - On the **Coding** toolbar, click the **Apply Comment** button and choose an option.
        - Choose **Apply HTML Comment** to enter an HTML comment.
        - Choose **Apply /* */ Comment** to insert a multiline comment.
        - Choose **Apply // Comment** to insert a single-line comment.
    - Choose **Insert→Comment** to insert a comment tag.
    - Or, right-click and choose **Selection** and then choose an HTML comment command.
4. Type the comment.
5. Save the web page.

Lesson 1: Working in Code View   19

Procedure Reference: Remove a Comment Tag

To remove a comment tag:

1. In Code view, select the comment tag.
2. On the **Coding** toolbar, click the **Remove Comment** button.

> Code can be commented to avoid being interpreted by the browser. Commented code can later be made executable by removing the comment tags.

3. Save the web page.

Procedure Reference: Enable Design Notes for a Site

To enable design notes for a site:

1. Display the **Manage Sites** dialog box.
2. In the **Manage Sites** dialog box, select a site and click **Edit.**
3. In the **Site Definition for <site name>** dialog box, select the **Advanced** tab.
4. In the **Category** list box, select **Design Notes.**
5. In the **Design Notes** section, check the **Maintain Design Notes** check box to enable design notes for all files on the site.
6. If necessary, click **Clean Up** to remove all the existing design notes from the site.
7. If necessary, check the **Upload Design Notes for Sharing** check box to transfer the design notes along with associated web pages when they are uploaded to a remote location.
8. Click **OK** to save the settings for the site.
9. In the **Manage Sites** dialog box, click **Done** to apply the changes to the specified site.

Procedure Reference: Add Design Notes

To add design notes:

1. Display the **Design Notes** dialog box.
   - Open the file for which the design note needs to be added and choose **File→Design Notes.**
   - In the **FILES** panel, select the required file, and from the **FILES** panel options menu, choose **File→Design Notes.**
   - Or, in the **FILES** panel, right-click the required file and choose **Design Notes.**

> The site where the file is saved must have the **Design Notes** option enabled.

2. If necessary, on the **Basic info** tab, from the **Status** drop-down list, select an option.
3. If necessary, above the **Notes** text box, click the **Insert date** button to insert the current date.
4. In the **Notes** text box, click and type the note.

5. If necessary, check the **Show when file is opened** check box to specify that the **Design Notes** dialog box be displayed whenever a user opens the file.
6. Select the **All info** tab and click the **Add item** button.
7. In the **Name** text box, type a name for the design note.
8. In the **Value** text box, type the note.
9. If necessary, click the **Add item** button to add more information.
10. If necessary, select a note and click the **Delete item** button to delete the selected information.
11. Click **OK** to save the design note.
12. Save and close the web page.
13. If necessary, view the design note.
    a. Open the web page.
    b. In the **Design Notes** dialog box, select the **All info** tab to view the contents of the design note.
    c. Click **OK** to close the design note.

Procedure Reference: Delete a Design Note Entry

To delete a design note:
1. Open a file and display the **Design Notes** dialog box.
2. In the **Design Notes** dialog box, select the **All info** tab.
3. In the **Info** list box, select the required note.
4. Click the **Delete item** button.
5. Click **OK.**

ACTIVITY 1-3
Adding Design Notes and Comments

Data Files:

clients.html

Before You Begin:

From the **FILES** panel, open the clients.html file.

Scenario:

Since your team members may work on this file, you want to include descriptions about code for the header image and image rollovers. You also realize that the Clients and Partners page needs to be updated. Since you are busy with other tasks, you want your colleague to replace the existing list of partners with an updated list.

What You Do	How You Do It
1. Insert comments on the page.	a. Switch to Code view. b. Click at the end of line 141, and press **Enter**. c. On the **Coding** toolbar, click the **Apply Comment** button, and choose **Apply HTML Comment**. d. In line 142, observe that an empty comment tag is inserted. e. Type *The following two lines define an image map on the header image* f. At the end of line 145, click and press **Enter**. g. On the **Coding** toolbar, click the **Apply Comment** button, and choose **Apply HTML Comment**. h. Type *The JavaScript functions used here are generated while creating image rollovers*

2. Add a design note to the page.

   a. Choose **File→Design Notes**.

   b. In the **Design Notes** dialog box, on the **Basic info** tab, from the **Status** drop-down list, select **needs attention.**

   c. In the **Notes** text box, click and type *Refer to the latest report from Corporate office for new partners and add them*

   d. Check the **Show when file is opened** check box.

   e. Select the **All info** tab and click the **Add Item** button to add more information to the design note.

   f. In the **Name** text box, type *Author* and press the **Tab** key.

   g. In the **Value** text box, type *OGC Design Team*

   h. In the **Design Notes** dialog box, click **OK.**

   i. Save and close the file.

3. View the design note.

   a. In the **FILES** panel, double-click **clients.html.**

   b. In the **Design Notes** dialog box, observe that a design note indicating that the partners list needs to be updated is displayed.

   c. Click **OK** to close the **Design Notes** dialog box.

   d. Close the file.

Lesson 1 Follow-up

In this lesson, you worked in Code view. Working in Code view enables you to modify web pages using coding tools and commands that Dreamweaver provides.

1. **Which coding tools and features do you find most useful? Why?**

2. **What information would you provide in the comments on your web pages?**

2 Formatting with Advanced CSS Techniques

Lesson Time: 1 hour(s), 40 minutes

Lesson Objectives:

In this lesson, you will format web pages using advanced CSS techniques.

You will:

- Create and apply external style sheets.
- Create a layout using CSS.
- Apply rollover effects using CSS.

Introduction

You worked in Code view and used the coding tools. You may now want to use advanced CSS techniques to control the appearance and layout of web pages. In this lesson, you will format content and lay out a web page using advanced CSS techniques.

When developing a website, it is important to ensure that pages load quickly and have consistent appearance with minimal code. Utilizing common code to define the layout and appearance of the pages of a site will help reduce the usage of code and enable making changes across pages simpler. Using advanced CSS techniques, you can achieve these easily.

TOPIC A
Use External Style Sheets

You worked in Code view to have greater control over the appearance of page elements. You may now want to use external style sheets to format the pages of your site. In this topic, you will create external style sheets and apply them to multiple pages.

Creating CSS styles to apply the same formatting to each web page on your site will be very tedious. Moreover, if you have to modify a particular style across the pages, it would mean redefining the style for each page. This not only takes a great deal of time, but also makes it difficult to ensure consistency. By using external style sheets, styles can be applied to multiple pages to ensure consistency.

Advanced Styles

Advanced styles are CSS styles that are used to redefine the formatting of elements when a Tag style or a Class style cannot be used. Dreamweaver provides four types of Advanced styles.

Type	Description
ID	Defines formatting for tags that contain a specific `id` attribute. IDs are different from classes because they are unique to a page. IDs are preceded by the pound (#) sign.
Pseudo-element	Defines formatting for subparts of an element. Pseudo-elements are frequently used for redefining the first letter or first line of a block of text.
Pseudo-class	Classifies elements on characteristics other than their name, attributes, or content. Pseudo-classes are frequently used for redefining the way links are displayed.
Combination	Redefines the formatting for a specific combination of two or more elements.

Default Style Sheets

Dreamweaver provides a set of sample style sheets, each containing various CSS rules. Depending on your needs, you can use any of the style sheets to apply formatting to your pages. These sample style sheets can also be used as a starting point, and by redefining the rules or adding more rules, a customized style sheet can be created. You can access the sample style sheets from the **New Document** dialog box or from the **Attach External Style Sheet** dialog box.

Advanced Selectors

Advanced CSS selectors help define CSS rules for elements based on their position in the document's markup, parent element, or attribute values. The following table describes the syntax of some commonly used CSS selectors.

Syntax	Description
*	The universal selector, which matches any element.
x	A tag selector, which matches any element of type x.
x y	A descendant selector, which matches any element y that is a descendant of the element x. The elements are separated by a space.
x>y	A child selector, which matches any element y that is a child of the element x.
x+y	An adjacent sibling selector, which matches any element y that immediately follows the element x.
x~y	A general sibling selector, which matches any element y that shares the same parent element as the element x.
x.classname	A class selector, which matches any element x with the specified class name.
x#idname	An ID selector, which matches any element x with the specified ID name.
x[attname]	An attribute selector, which matches any element x with the specified attribute.
x[attname="attvalue"]	An attribute selector, which matches any element x with the specified attribute and its value.
x: first-line	A pseudo-element selector, which matches the first line of an element x.
x: first-letter	A pseudo-element selector, which matches the first letter of an element x.
x:link	A link pseudo-class selector, which matches any element x that is a source hyperlink not yet visited.
x:visited	A link pseudo-class selector, which matches any element x that is a source hyperlink already visited.
x:first-child	A pseudo-class selector, which matches any element x that is a first child of its parent element.
x:first-of-type	A pseudo-class selector, which matches any element x that is a first sibling of its type.

Inheritance and Specificity

Inheritance is a process by which CSS properties applied to an element are also applied to other elements nested within it. It is based on the nesting hierarchy of XHTML elements on a web page. Descendant elements can inherit properties of any ancestor element. This removes the need to declare properties repeatedly in a style sheet. However, not all properties are inheritable. In general, most text and font properties can be inherited, while properties that affect positioning such as margin, padding, and border are not inherited.

Specificity is a method for determining which rules apply to an element based on identifying which selectors are more specific than others. This is important when the same property with different values is applied to an element through different selectors. Specificity can be determined by using the following process.

1. A property assigned through a style has maximum specificity. Thus, inline declarations have more specificity than a rule with selectors, and are always applied to the element. If no inline declarations are present, proceed to the next step.

2. Determine the number of ID selectors for all the rule declarations that affect the element. The declaration with the most ID selectors has the highest specificity and is applied to the element. If two or more declarations are tied with the highest number of ID selectors, proceed to the next step.

3. Determine the number of class selectors, pseudo classes, and attribute selectors for all the rule declarations that are tied in the previous step. The declaration with the highest count has the highest specificity and is applied to the element. If two or more declarations are tied with the highest count, proceed to the next step.

4. Determine the number of tag selectors and pseudo elements for all the rule declarations that are tied in the previous step. The declaration with the highest count has the highest specificity and is applied to the element. If two or more declarations are tied with the highest count, proceed to the next step.

5. For rule declarations that are tied after the previous steps, the rule that is declared later takes precedence.

Style Overriding

When multiple style sheets contain the same style rule, the style that is defined closest to the element is the one that gets applied. In other words, inline styles that are closest to the element override embedded styles, which in turn override external styles. So, if an external style sheet and an embedded style sheet both apply different values to the same property of an element, the values specified in the embedded style overrides the values in the external style sheet. Similarly, inline styles override embedded and external style sheets.

The order in which styles are placed is also a key factor in style sheet precedence. If a `<link>` tag is placed after the `<style>` section of an embedded style sheet, the external style sheet takes precedence. When multiple external style sheets are linked, the last one takes higher precedence. Similarly, if two rules use the same property for the same selector, the second rule overrides the first rule.

Methods of Attaching External Style Sheets

An external style sheet can be attached to a web page either by linking or importing it. When an external style sheet is linked, a `<link>` tag is inserted in the head section of the web page, establishing a link to the external style sheet. When imported, the external style sheet is embedded with the style sheets on the web page using the `@import` rule placed within the `<style>` tag. You can import one style sheet into another. Whether linked or imported, changes made to the external style sheet will affect all the web pages it is attached to.

Related Files

Related files are files, such as CSS and JavaScript files, that are associated with the current document. The **Related Files** toolbar displays all the related files and allows you to access them. Using this toolbar, you can open any related file to view and edit its content, while keeping the main document open. The **Related Files** toolbar displays files such as client side scripts, server side includes, Spry data sources, JavaScript files, and external style sheets. The toolbar appears only if there are external files associated with the current document.

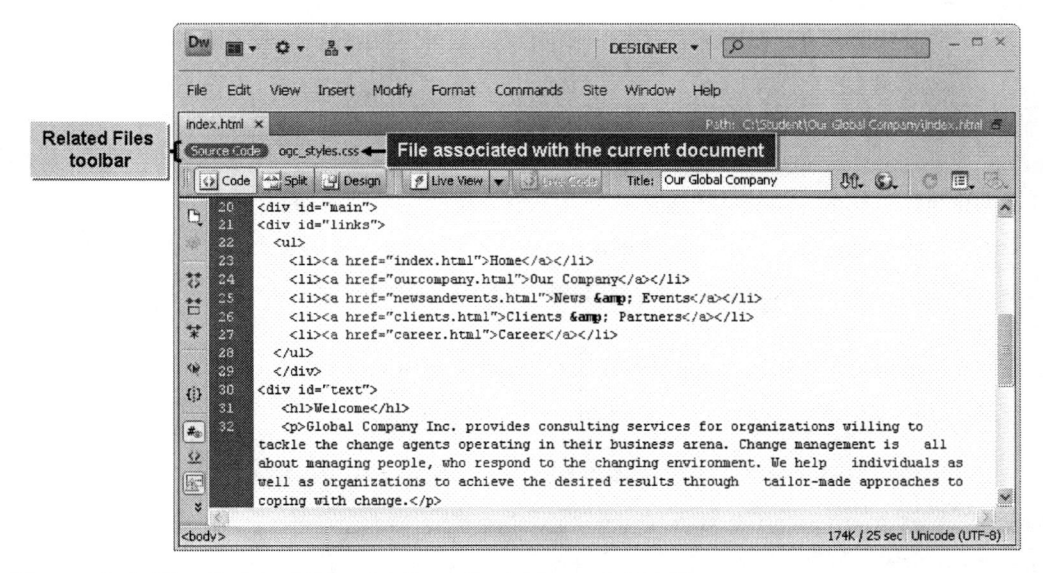

Figure 2-1: The Related Files toolbar displaying related files.

How to Use External Style Sheets

Procedure Reference: Create an External Style Sheet

To create an external style sheet:
1. Choose **File→New.**
2. If necessary, in the **New Document** dialog box, select the **Blank Page** tab.
3. In the **Page Type** list box, select **CSS.**
4. Click **Create.**
5. Using the **CSS STYLES** panel, add CSS rules to the external style sheet.
6. Save the file.

Procedure Reference: Attach an External Style Sheet to a Web Page

To attach an external style sheet to a web page:
1. Open the web page to which the external style sheet has to be attached.
2. Display the **Attach External Style Sheet** dialog box.
    - At the bottom of the **CSS STYLES** panel, click the **Attach Style Sheet** button.
    - Or, from the **CSS STYLES** panel options menu, choose **Attach Style Sheet.**
3. To the right of the **File/URL** text box, click **Browse,** navigate to the location where the external style sheet is stored, and select the external style sheet.
4. In the **Add as** section, select an option.
    - Select **Link** to create a link between the document and the external style sheet.
    - Select **Import** to attach the external style sheet to the document as an import directive.
5. If necessary, from the **Media** drop-down list, select a media type.
6. Click **OK** to attach the external style sheet to the document.

Procedure Reference: Export CSS Rules to an External Style Sheet

To export CSS rules to an external style sheet:
1. If necessary, open the **CSS STYLES** panel to display the available styles.
2. Select the CSS rules to be exported.
3. Display the **Move To External Style Sheet** dialog box.
    - From the **CSS STYLES** panel options menu, choose **Move CSS Rules.**
    - Or, right-click the selected styles and choose **Move CSS Rules.**
4. In the **Move Rules To** section, select an option.
    - Move the selected rules to an existing external style sheet.
        a. Select **Style sheet.**
        b. Specify the external style sheet to which the rules are to be moved.
            - To the right of the **Style sheet** option, in the text box, type the path and name of the external style sheet.
            - Or, click **Browse,** and in the **Select Style Sheet File** dialog box, navigate to the required folder, and select the file.
        c. Click **OK** to move the rules.
    - Move the selected rules to a new external style sheet.

a. Select **A new style sheet** and click **OK.**
b. If necessary, in the **Save Style Sheet File As** dialog box, navigate to a folder.
c. In the **File name** text box, type a name for the external style sheet.
d. Click **Save.**

Procedure Reference: Unlink an External Style Sheet

To unlink an external style sheet:
1. In the **CSS STYLES** panel, select an external style sheet.
2. At the bottom of the **CSS STYLES** panel, click the **Unlink CSS Stylesheet** button.

ACTIVITY 2-1
Creating External Style Sheets

Data Files:

clients.html, ogc_styles.css

Before You Begin:
1. From the **FILES** panel, open the clients.html file.
2. Close the **Design Notes** dialog box.
3. Switch to Design view.

Scenario:

You want to have a set of common CSS rules that can be applied to all pages of your website to ensure consistent formatting. You feel that modifying the CSS rules in each page is becoming tedious whenever you need to change the appearance across the site. Instead, you want to be able to make changes in a single file that can be applied to all the pages of your site.

What You Do	How You Do It
1. Create a CSS rule in an external style sheet.	a. Double-click the **CSS STYLES** tab to expand the **CSS STYLES** panel. b. At the bottom of the **CSS STYLES** panel, click the **New CSS Rule** button. c. In the **New CSS Rule** dialog box, in the **Selector Type** section, from the drop-down list, select **Tag (redefines an HTML element)**. d. In the **Selector Name** section, in the drop-down list, scroll up and select **body**. e. In the **Rule Definition** section, from the drop-down list, select **(New Style Sheet File)** and click **OK**. f. In the **File name** text box, type *ogc_styles* and click **Save** to save the CSS file.

2. Add properties for the CSS rule.

   a. In the **CSS Rule Definition for body in ogc_styles.css** dialog box, from the **Font-family** drop-down list, select **Arial, Helvetica, sans-serif.**

   b. In the **Category** list box, select **Block.**

   c. From the **Text-align** drop-down list, select **justify.**

   d. Click **OK** to add the CSS rule.

   e. Observe that the **Related Files** toolbar is displayed with the file ogc_styles.css.

3. Create a compound tag style for the body, para, and heading tags.

   a. On the **Related Files** toolbar, click **ogc_styles.css.**

   b. Observe that the document window switches to Split view, displaying the ogc_styles.css file in Code view and the source file in Design view.

   c. In Code view, in line 2, click after the word "body," and type **, p, h1, h2, h3, h4, h5, h6** to specify the same style for these tags as well.

   d. In the **CSS STYLES** panel, click **Refresh** to reflect the change made in the external style sheet.

   e. In the **CSS STYLES** panel, click **All** to display all the rules in the external style sheet.

4. Move a CSS rule to the external style sheet.

   a. On the **Related Files** toolbar, click **Source Code.**

   b. In the **CSS STYLES** panel, in the **All Rules** list box, scroll up and select the **h1** rule.

   c. From the **CSS STYLES** panel options menu, choose **Move CSS Rules.**

   d. In the **Move To External Style Sheet** dialog box, verify that the **Style sheet** option is selected, and in the drop-down list, verify that **ogc_styles.css** is selected.

   e. Click **OK.**

   f. In the **CSS STYLES** panel, observe that the **h1** rule is moved to the **ogc_styles.css** sub-tree.

   g. Save all the open files.

ACTIVITY 2-2
Applying an External Style Sheet

Data Files:

clients.html, index.html, ogc_styles.css

Before You Begin:

1. The clients.html file is open.
2. Switch to Design view.

Scenario:

You need to add a few CSS rules to most of the pages on the website. However, you already have these rules in an external style sheet. Instead of adding the CSS rules on each page, you want to use the CSS rules that you have in the external style sheet for other pages.

What You Do	How You Do It
1. Remove the h1 style.	a. In the **FILES** panel, scroll down and double-click **index.html.**
	b. Observe the formatting applied to the heading text "Welcome".
	c. In the **CSS STYLES** panel, in the **All Rules** section, select **h1** and click the **Delete CSS Rule** button, to delete the h1 rule.
	d. Observe that the default formatting is applied to the heading text "Welcome".
2. Attach the external style sheet to the home page.	a. At the bottom of the **CSS STYLES** panel, click the **Attach Style Sheet** button.
	b. In the **Attach External Style Sheet** dialog box, click **Browse**.
	c. Select the **ogc_styles.css** file and click **OK.**
	d. In the **Add as** section, verify that **Link** is selected and click **OK** to attach the style sheet to the web page.
	e. Observe that ogc_styles.css is now displayed on the **Related Files** toolbar.

3.	Edit the external style sheet.	a.	On the **Related Files** toolbar, click **ogc_styles.css.**
		b.	Observe that the ogc_styles.css style sheet is displayed in Code view and the index.html file is displayed in Design view.
		c.	In Code view, in the line number section, click **8** to select the entire line.
		d.	Press **Delete** to delete the font-family property declaration, because it is already declared in the previous rule.
		e.	In line **9,** select the color value **"#999"** and type *"#369"* to specify a new color for the heading.
4.	Check whether the redefined style is applied to all pages.	a.	On the **Related Files** toolbar, click **Source Code** to switch to the index.html file.
		b.	Switch to Design view.
		c.	Observe that the color of the heading text has changed.
		d.	Select the **clients.html** tab to switch to the clients.html file.
		e.	Observe that the new color is applied to the heading text on this page.
		f.	Save and close all the files.

TOPIC B
Create a Layout Using CSS

You created external style sheets and applied them to your pages. You now want to lay out a page to position its elements. In this topic, you will create a page layout using CSS.

While inserting elements on a web page, you may have difficulty in placing them at the required position. It would be easy if you could divide your page into portions and place page elements in the required areas. Using CSS, you will be able to position elements precisely in defined containers and also control how they appear on the web page.

ID Styles

ID styles are CSS styles applied to a single instance of an element on a web page. They are identified by names prefixed with a pound sign (#). You can apply this style to any element by specifying the name of the ID style in the `id` attribute. ID styles are most commonly used when creating page layouts with CSS to apply formatting to `<div>` tags. ID styles can be defined in either an embedded style sheet or in an attached external style sheet.

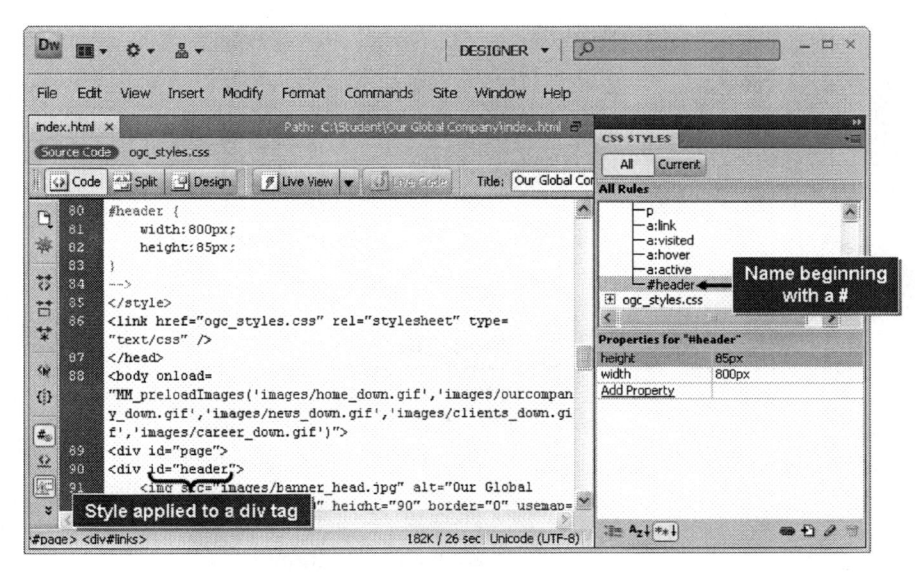

Figure 2-2: An ID style used to format a div tag.

CSS Layout Block

A *CSS layout block* is an HTML element that is represented as a rectangular box. It is used to position content on a web page. Each layout block element contains a content area that is surrounded by padding, border, and margins. There are two types of layout elements: block and inline. While block elements can contain inline elements and other block-level elements, inline elements can contain only other inline elements.

CSS Layouts

A CSS web page layout is built by applying CSS properties to `<div>` tags to position, size, and align them. You can add a number of `<div>` tags and position them using CSS to suit your layout requirements. The border, padding, margin, and background color properties are some of the commonly used properties to define the appearance of div containers. CSS layouts are built as either fixed layouts or fluid layouts. Fixed layouts are those in which dimensions are set in pixels to retain their original dimensions even when the browser is resized. Fluid layouts are those in which dimensions are set in percentages to resize the containers along with the browser window.

CSS Layout Box Model

The *CSS Layout Box model* is a visual aid that displays the box model of the currently selected CSS layout block. It visually displays the padding and margins around the layout block. The values associated with the padding and margin attributes appear in a tooltip when you move the mouse pointer over any of the edges of the layout block.

CSS Layout Outlines

CSS Layout Outlines is a visual aid that displays the outlines of the CSS layout blocks in Design view. The outlines appear as dashed lines for `<div>` elements and solid lines for AP (Absolutely Positioned) elements. Clicking an outline allows you to select the CSS layout block.

The position Property

The `position` property is used to specify how an element is positioned on a web page. However, the actual coordinates are specified using the `left`, `right`, `top`, and `bottom` properties.

The table describes the values that can be assigned to the `position` property.

Value	Description
static	Positions the element at its location specified in the flow of code on the web page. It does not take any value for left, right, top, or bottom positions. This is the default value assigned to all elements.
absolute	Positions the element at the specified coordinates relative to the top-left corner of its container.
fixed	Positions the element at the specified coordinates relative to the top-left corner of the browser window. The element will remain in the same position even when the page is scrolled.
relative	Positions the element relative to the location it would usually take in the flow of content on the web page. For example, `top: 30 px;` adds 30 pixels to the top of the element when it is positioned after the previous element on the page.

Measurement Units in CSS

Measurement units for CSS properties can be classified under three categories: relative, absolute, or percentage.

The table describes the classifications the units fall under.

Classification	Description
Relative	Units are assigned values relative to other values. This allows you to render the element in a flexible manner. Relative units used in CSS are em, ex, and px.
Absolute	Units are assigned absolute values. Specifying properties with absolute units renders the elements in a rigid manner. Absolute units used in CSS are pt, pc, in, cm, and mm.
Percentage	Units are assigned values as a percentage of the values inherited from the parent element. Percentage units are specified using the percent (%) symbol.

How to Create a Layout Using CSS

Procedure Reference: Create an ID Style

To create an ID style:

1. If necessary, choose **Window→CSS Styles** to display the **CSS STYLES** panel.
2. Display the **New CSS Rule** dialog box.
   - At the bottom of the **CSS STYLES** panel, click the **New CSS Rule** button.
   - Or, from the **CSS STYLES** panel options menu, choose **New.**
3. From the **Selector Type** drop-down list, select **ID (applies to only one HTML element).**
4. In the **Selector Name** section, in the **Choose or enter a name for your selector** text box, type a name for the ID style.
5. From the **Rule Definition** drop-down list, select the location where the styles are to be saved.
6. Click **OK.**
7. In the **CSS Rule definition for <rule name>** dialog box, in the **Category** list box, select a category.
8. In the selected category, set the values of the properties.
9. Click **Apply** to add the CSS rule.
10. Click **OK.**

Procedure Reference: Create a Page Layout Using CSS

To create a CSS page layout:

1. If necessary, select the content.
2. Insert a `<div>` container.

3. Define an ID style with the necessary properties.
   - Add declarations to set the positioning properties.
   - Add declarations to set the size.
   - Add declarations to set the alignment.
   - Add declarations to control the appearance.
4. Apply the ID style to the `<div>` container.
5. If necessary, move the content to the `<div>` container.
6. If necessary, add more `<div>` containers and format them with ID styles.
7. Save the file.

Procedure Reference: Format a Menu Using CSS

To format a menu using CSS:
1. Create an unordered list for the menu.
2. Create a CSS rule to format the `<ul>` tag.
3. For the `list-style` attribute, assign the value `none` to not display any bullets.
4. If necessary, add CSS properties to modify the appearance of list items.
   - For the `display` attribute, assign the value `list-item` to display the links as a list.
   - For the `display` attribute, assign the value `inline` to display the links horizontally in a single line.
   - For the `list-style-position` attribute, assign the value `outside` to alter the indentation of the list item.

ACTIVITY 2-3
Creating a Page Layout Using CSS

Data Files:

newproducts.html

Before You Begin:

From the **FILES** panel, open the newproducts.html file.

Scenario:

Your manager has asked you to enhance the look and feel of the website. You feel that a new design with proper positioning of elements will help to enhance the appearance of the page and also present information effectively. You want to use CSS to accurately position the elements.

What You Do	How You Do It
1. Insert a container for the header image.	a. In the **INSERT** panel, click **Insert Div Tag**. b. In the **Insert Div Tag** dialog box, from the **Insert** drop-down list, select **After start of tag.** c. In the drop-down list to the right of the **Insert** drop-down list, verify that **\<body\>** is selected. d. In the **ID** text box, click and type *header* and then click **OK**.

Adobe® Dreamweaver® CS4: Level 2

2. Create an ID style for the header.

    a. At the bottom of the **CSS STYLES** panel, click the **New CSS Rule** button.

    b. In the **New CSS Rule** dialog box, in the **Selector Type** section, in the drop-down list, verify that **ID (applies to only one HTML element)** is selected.

    c. In the **Selector Name** section, in the **Choose or enter a name for your selector** drop-down list, verify that **#header** is selected.

    d. In the **Rule Definition** section, in the drop-down list, verify that **ogc_styles.css** is selected and click **OK**.

    e. In the **CSS Rule definition for #header in ogc_styles.css** dialog box, in the **Category** list box, select **Box**.

    f. In the **Width** text box, type *800*

    g. In the **Height** text box, type *90*

    h. Click **OK** to apply the ID style to the header container.

3. Insert containers for the news headlines and main content on the web page.

    a. In the **INSERT** panel, click **Insert Div Tag**.

    b. In the **Insert Div Tag** dialog box, from the **Insert** drop-down list, select **After tag.**

    c. In the drop-down list to the right of the **Insert** drop-down list, verify that **<div id="header">** is selected.

    d. In the **ID** text box, type *news* and click **OK.**

    e. Click before the text "Home", hold down **Shift,** and in the last line, click at the end of the text "products are:".

    f. In the **INSERT** panel, click **Insert Div Tag.**

    g. In the **Insert Div Tag** dialog box, in the **Insert** drop-down list, verify that **Wrap around selection** is selected.

    h. In the **ID** text box, type *main* and then click **OK.**

    i. Observe that a container is inserted with the selected text.

Lesson 2: Formatting with Advanced CSS Techniques

4. Create ID styles for the news and main containers.

    a. On the **Related Files** toolbar, click **ogc_styles.css.**

    b. Verify that the insertion point is placed in line 15.

    c. Switch to Code view.

    d. Type `#news {` and press **Enter** to start defining an ID style for the news container.

    e. Type `height: 20px;` and press **Enter.**

    f. Type `width: 800px;` and press **Enter.**

    g. Type `}` and press **Enter** to complete the CSS rule.

    h. Similarly, create an ID style named *#main* with **height** of *500px* and **width** of *800px*

5. Insert a container for the footer.

    a. On the **Related Files** toolbar, click **Source Code** and switch to Design view.

    b. In the document window, scroll down and click below the main container.

    c. In the **INSERT** panel, click **Insert Div Tag**.

    d. In the **Insert Div Tag** dialog box, from the **Insert** drop-down list, select **After tag.**

    e. From the drop-down list to the right of the **Insert** drop-down list, select **<div id="main">.**

    f. In the **ID** text box, click and type *footer*

Lesson 2: Formatting with Advanced CSS Techniques   **45**

6. Create an ID style for the footer.

   a. Click **New CSS Rule.**

   b. In the **New CSS Rule** dialog box, in the **Selector Name** section, in the **Choose or enter a name for your selector** drop-down list, verify that **#footer** is selected and click **OK.**

   c. In the **CSS Rule Definition for #footer in ogc_styles.css** dialog box, in the **Category** list box, select **Box.**

   d. In the **Width** text box, type *800*

   e. In the **Height** text box, type *40* and click **OK.**

   f. In the **Insert Div Tag** dialog box, click **OK.**

7. Split the main container into three sub-containers.

   a. In the document window, scroll up, and in the main container, click before the word "Home", hold down **Shift,** and click after the word "Career" to select the links.

   b. In the **INSERT** panel, click **Insert Div Tag.**

   c. In the **Insert Div Tag** dialog box, in the **Insert** drop-down list, verify that **Wrap around selection** is selected, and in the **ID** text box, type *links* and click **OK.**

   d. In the main container, click before the text "New Products", hold down **Shift,** and click after the text "products are:" to select the text.

   e. Insert a `<div>` tag to wrap around the selected text with the **ID** name *text*

   f. Insert a `<div>` tag after the tag `<div id="text">`, with the **ID** name *images*

Adobe® Dreamweaver® CS4: Level 2

8. Create ID styles to position the sub-containers.

   a. On the **Related Files** toolbar, click **ogc_styles.css.**

   b. Verify that the insertion point is placed in line 28.

   c. Switch to Code view.

   d. Create an ID style named **links** with a width of 120 pixels, a height of 500 pixels, and the float set to left.

   See Code Sample 1.

   e. Press **Enter.**

   f. Create an ID style named **text** with a width of 410 pixels, a height of 500 pixels, float set to left, and a padding of 10 pixels on the left and right.

   See Code Sample 2.

   g. Press **Enter.**

   h. Create an ID style named **images** with a width of 250 pixels, a height of 500 pixels, and float set to right.

   See Code Sample 3.

   i. On the **Related Files** toolbar, click **Source Code.**

   j. Switch to Design view.

   k. Observe that the three containers are placed within the main container beside each other.

   l. Save all the open files.

Code Sample 1

```
#main #links {
width: 120px;
height: 500px;
float: left;
}
```

Code Sample 2

```
#main #text {
width: 410px;
height: 500px;
float: left;
```

Lesson 2: Formatting with Advanced CSS Techniques   **47**

```
padding-left: 10px;
padding-right: 10px;
}
```

Code Sample 3

```
#main #images {
width: 250px;
height: 500px;
float: right;
}
```

ACTIVITY 2-4
Formatting a Page Layout Using CSS

Data Files:
newproducts.html, ogc_styles.css

Before You Begin:
The newproducts.html file is open.

Scenario:
You want to enhance the formatting of the content within each container. You also need to enhance the overall visual appeal of the layout.

What You Do	How You Do It
1. Create a CSS rule for the body tag.	a. At the bottom of the **CSS STYLES** panel, click the **New CSS Rule** button.
	b. In the **New CSS Rule** dialog box, in the **Selector Type** section, from the drop-down list, select **Tag (redefines an HTML element).**
	c. If necessary, in the **Selector Name** section, in the **Choose or enter a name for your selector** drop-down list, scroll up and select **body.**
	d. In the **Rule Definition** section, in the drop-down list, verify that **ogc_styles.css** is selected and click **OK.**

Adobe® Dreamweaver® CS4: Level 2

2.	Specify CSS properties for a background image.	a.	In the **CSS Rule Definition for body in ogc_styles.css** dialog box, in the **Category** list box, select **Background**.
		b.	To the right of the **Background-image** drop-down list, click **Browse**.
		c.	In the **Select Image Source** dialog box, navigate to the C:\084054Data\Our Global Company\images folder.
		d.	Select **body_background_image.jpg** and click **OK**.
		e.	From the **Background-repeat** drop-down list, select **repeat**.
		f.	In the **Category** list box, select **Box**.
		g.	In the **Padding** section, verify that the **Same for all** check box is checked, and in the **Top** text box, click and type *0*
		h.	In the **Margin** section, verify that the **Same for all** check box is checked, and in the **Top** text box, type *0*
		i.	Click **OK** to add the CSS rule.
		j.	Observe that a background pattern is visible for the entire page.
3.	Add an image to the header container.	a.	In the document window, in the header container, select the text **"Content for id "header" Goes Here"**, and press **Delete**.
		b.	Choose **Insert→Image**.
		c.	In the **Select Image Source** dialog box, select **banner_head.jpg** and click **OK**.
		d.	In the **Image Tag Accessibility Attributes** dialog box, in the **Alternate text** text box, type *Our Global Company Header* and click **OK**.

4. Add a background color for the news container and the sub-containers.

    a. On the **Related Files** toolbar, click **ogc_styles.css** and switch to Code view.

    b. Scroll up, click at the end of line 29 and press **Enter.**

    c. Type **background-color: #CCC;** to set the background color for the news container.

    d. If necessary, scroll down to line 34.

    e. Click at the end of line 34 and press **Enter.**

    f. Type **background-color: #FFF;** to set the background color for the main container.

    g. Similarly, in the CSS rules for the links container and the images container, after the float property, add the background color property with the values *#B5D4EB* and *#8E8E8E* respectively.

    See Code Sample 1.

    See Code Sample 2.

Code Sample 1

```
#main #links {
width: 1200px;
height: 500px;
float: left;
background-color: #B5D4EB;
}
```

Code Sample 2

```
#main #images {
width: 250px;
height: 500px;
float: right;
background-color: #8E8E8E;
}
```

5. Add CSS properties for the footer container.

   a. Double-click the **INSERT** tab to minimize the **INSERT** panel.

   b. In the **CSS STYLES** panel, click **Refresh** and in the **All Rules** section, select **#footer**.

   c. In the **Properties for "#footer"** pane, click **Add Property,** and in the drop-down list, scroll down and select **padding-top.**

   d. In the text box to the right of the **padding-top** property, type *0*

   e. Similarly, add the **font-size** property with the value *10* and the **background-color** property with the value *#4C70A2* and the **text-align** property with the value *center*

6. Center align the page.

   a. Scroll to the top of the Code view, click at the end of line 1, and press **Enter.**

   b. Create an ID style named *wrapper* with a margin of 0 pixels and a width of 800 pixels.

   See Code Sample 3.

   c. On the **Related Files** toolbar, click **Source Code.**

   d. In line 11, click after the `<body>` tag, press **Enter** and type `<div id="wrapper">`

   e. Scroll down, click at the end of line 29, and press **Enter.**

   f. Type `</` to close the `<div>` tag.

Code Sample 3

```
#wrapper {
margin: 0px auto;
width: 800px;
}
```

7. Format the links.

    a. Switch to Design view.

    b. In the document window, scroll up, and in the links container, in the first line, click before the word "Home", hold down **Shift,** and in the last line, click after the word "Career".

    c. In the **Property Inspector,** click the **Unordered List** button to format the links as an unordered list.

    d. On the **Related Files** toolbar, click **ogc_style.css.**

    e. Switch to Code view.

    f. Scroll down to the bottom of Code view and click in line 64.

    g. Create a CSS rule to format the unordered list with the Arial font family, a font size of 12 pixels, margins and padding of 0 pixels, a width of 110 pixels, and the list style type set to none.

    See Code Sample 4.

    h. Create a CSS rule to format the list items with display set to list-item, a height of 20 pixels, a width of 120 pixels, padding-top set to 5 pixels, padding-bottom set to 0 pixels, list style position set to outside, and a line height of 35 pixels.

    See Code Sample 5.

Code Sample 4

```
#wrapper #main #links ul {
font-family: Arial, Helvetica, sans-serif;
font-size: 12px;
margin: 0px;
padding: 0px;
list-style-type: none;
width: 110px;
}
```

Code Sample 5

```
#wrapper #main #links ul li {
display: list-item;
height: 20px;
width: 120px;
padding-top: 5px;
padding-bottom: 0px;
list-style-position: outside;
```

```
line-height: 35px;
}
```

8. Preview the page in a browser.

    a. Save all the files.

    b. Preview the page in Internet Explorer.

    c. Maximize the Internet Explorer window.

    d. Observe that the web page is centered in the browser.

    e. Close the Internet Explorer window.

TOPIC C
Apply Rollover Effects Using CSS

You created a page layout using CSS. You may now want to provide a visually appealing navigation interface. In this topic, you will apply rollover effects using CSS.

Providing a navigation interface to your web pages with rollover effects will make your pages more attractive. Rollover effects created with images normally require the use of multiple images and more code resulting in slower download times. Ideally, you will want to use lesser images and minimal code while retaining the same visual appeal. You can achieve this using CSS.

How to Apply Rollover Effects Using CSS
Procedure Reference: Create a Rollover Effect for Links Using CSS

To create a rollover effect for links using CSS:

1. If necessary, modify the CSS properties of the `<ul>` and `<li>` tags to format the menu.
2. Modify the appearance of links for the normal state.
    a. Create a CSS rule for the `<a>` tags within the list.
    b. Specify the CSS properties for the links.
        - For the `color` attribute, specify a value to set the font color.
        - For the `text-decoration` attribute, specify the value `none` to display the links without underlining.
        - For the `background-image` attribute, specify a background image.
        - For the `background-repeat` attribute, specify the value `none` to avoid background repetition.
        - For the `background-position` attribute, specify the X and Y coordinates to set the position of the background image.
    c. If necessary, specify the properties to position the links.
3. Create a CSS rule for the rollover effect.
    a. Create a CSS rule for the `a:hover` pseudo-class.
    b. Specify the CSS properties to alter the appearance of the link when the mouse pointer is hovered over it.

> Text properties such as the font family, font size, or font color can be varied to provide the rollover effect. Different background images can also be specified for different states to create the rollover effect.

4. Save the page.
5. Preview the page in a browser.

ACTIVITY 2-5
Applying Rollover Effects Using CSS

Data Files:

newproducts.html, ogc_styles.css

Before You Begin:
1. The newproducts.html file is open.
2. On the **Related Files** toolbar, click **Source Code**.
3. Switch to Design view.

Scenario:

You prepared a new layout for the website. Before presenting it to your manager, you want to add a fully functional navigation menu that also looks visually appealing.

What You Do	How You Do It
1. Add a CSS rule for the links.	a. In the links container, click the word **"Home"**.
	b. On the status bar, in the tag selector, select **\<a\>**.
	c. At the bottom of the **CSS STYLES** panel, click the **New CSS Rule** button.
	d. In the **New CSS Rule** dialog box, in the **Selector Name** section, in the **Choose or enter a name for your selector** drop-down list, verify that **#wrapper #main #links ul li a** is selected and click **OK**.

2. Specify CSS properties for the links in normal state.

   a. In the **Color** text box, type **#000**

   b. In the **Text-decoration** section, check the **none** check box.

   c. In the **Category** list box, select **Background.**

   d. To the right of the **Background-image** drop-down list, click **Browse.**

   e. If necessary, in the **Select Image Source** dialog box, navigate to the C:\084054Data\ Our Global Company\images folder.

   f. Scroll to the right, select **up_img.jpg** and click **OK.**

   g. From the **Background-repeat** drop-down list, select **no-repeat.**

   h. In the **Background-position (X)** text box, type **0**

   i. In the **Background-position (Y)** text box, type **5**

3. Add the block and box CSS properties for the links.

   a. In the **Category** list box, select **Block.**

   b. From the **Display** drop-down list, select **list-item.**

   c. In the **Category** list box, select **Box.**

   d. In the **Width** text box, type **110**

   e. In the **Padding** section, uncheck the **Same for all** check box.

   f. In the **Left** text box, type **10**

   g. Click **OK** to add the CSS rule.

4. Apply a rollover effect to the links.

    a. In the **CSS STYLES** panel, in the **All Rules** section, verify that the **#wrapper #main #links ul li a** rule is selected.

    b. From the **CSS STYLES** panel options menu, choose **Duplicate** to make a copy of the selected CSS rule.

    c. In the **Duplicate CSS Rule** dialog box, in the **Selector Name** section, in the **Choose or enter a name for your selector** text box, place the insertion point at the end and type *:hover*

    d. In the **Rule Definition** section, in the drop-down list, verify that **ogc_styles.css** is selected and click **OK**.

    e. In the **CSS STYLES** panel, in the **All Rules** section, scroll to the bottom and select the **#wrapper #main #links ul li a:hover** rule.

    f. In the **Properties for "#wrapper #main #links ul li a:hover"** pane, click in the text box to the right of the **background-image** property, and to the right of the text box, click the **Browse** button.

    g. In the **Select Image Source** dialog box, scroll to the right, select **down_img.jpg** and click **OK**.

    h. Click in the text box to the right of the **color** property, type *#FFF* and press **Enter**.

5. Preview the web page in a browser.

    a. Save all the files.

    b. Preview the web page in Internet Explorer.

    c. Move the mouse pointer over the "Home" link to view the rollover effect.

    d. Close the Internet Explorer window.

    e. Close the file.

> A different set of files will be used for the activities from the next lesson. If you need a copy of the files you worked on, make a backup of the C:\084054Data\Our Global Company folder.

Lesson 2 Follow-up

In this lesson, you used advanced CSS techniques to control the appearance and layout of web pages. This allows you to enhance the appearance of web pages and also optimize pages, enabling faster downloads and uniform formatting across the site.

1. **How would you use CSS to enhance your website?**

2. **Which CSS styles would you save in external style sheets? Why?**

3 | Working with AP Elements

Lesson Time: 55 minutes

Lesson Objectives:

In this lesson, you will work with AP elements.

You will:
- Create AP elements.
- Control AP elements.

Introduction

You used CSS to format and lay out your web pages. You now want to improve the presentation of the web pages by accurately positioning elements within them and enhancing the layout. In this lesson, you will create and control AP elements.

Managing the positioning of elements on complex web pages could be difficult. By using AP elements, you can overcome this and precisely position elements on a web page however complex they are.

TOPIC A
Create AP Elements

You used CSS to add rollover effects to elements on web pages. You may now want to employ a layout mechanism that helps you position page elements on top of each other. In this topic, you will create AP elements.

When designing a web page, you may need to insert elements, such as text and images, at specific locations on the web page. You may want to place some page elements over other elements. Creating AP elements will help you achieve this without affecting the page layout.

AP Elements

Definition:

An Absolutely Positioned element (*AP element*) is a block-level HTML element that is described by an absolute position and exact dimensions. It can contain text, images, and other page elements, and can be positioned anywhere on the web page. You can place an AP element in front of or behind other AP elements and also control its visibility. Each AP element is distinguished from the others by its name and stacking order.

Example:

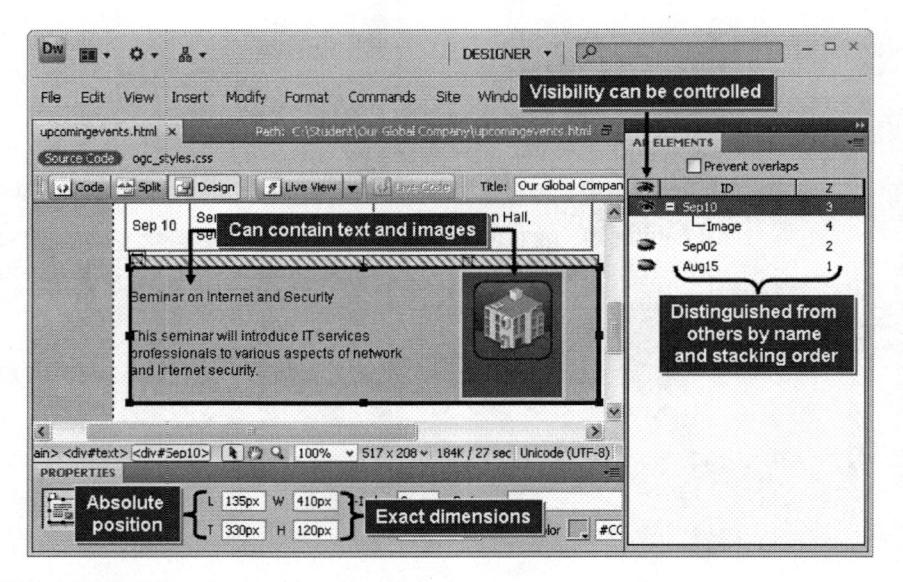

Figure 3-1: AP elements inserted on a web page.

Positioning of AP Elements

The position of AP elements on a web page can be specified using the values `absolute`, `relative`, `fixed`, or `static` for the `position` attribute. When a new AP element is inserted, the default positioning method used is absolute positioning.

The AP ELEMENTS Panel

The **AP ELEMENTS** panel allows you to manipulate AP elements by hiding or displaying them, thereby preventing overlap of content, modifying the stacking order, and selecting one or more AP elements. It has three columns; the first column, denoted by an eye icon, is used to control the visibility of the AP elements; the second column, called **ID,** identifies the AP elements by their names; the third column, called **Z,** displays the stacking order of the AP elements.

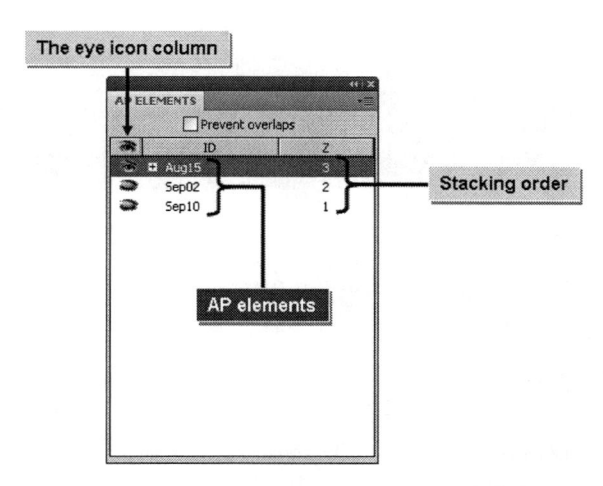

Figure 3-2: The AP ELEMENTS panel displaying a list of AP elements on a web page.

Stacking Order

Stacking order, referred to as the **Z-Index,** is a property of AP elements. It determines the order in which AP elements appear on a web page. While the first created AP element assumes a stacking order of 1, the most recently created AP element assumes the highest stacking order. The AP element with the highest stacking order appears in front of the other AP elements. The **AP ELEMENTS** panel lists AP elements in increasing order of their stacking order.

How to Create AP Elements

Procedure Reference: Create an AP Element

To create an AP element:

1. Insert an AP element.
   - Position the insertion point at a location and choose **Insert→Layout Objects→AP Div.**

   > When AP elements are added to a page using the **Insert** menu, the inserted AP element is always in a default size. The default size in Dreamweaver is a width of 200px and height of 115px. This default size for AP elements can be changed in the **Preferences** dialog box, in the **AP elements** category.

   - Or, draw the AP element using the **Draw AP Div** button.
     a. In the **INSERT** panel, from the drop-down list, select **Layout.**
     b. Click **Draw AP Div.**
     c. In the document window, click at a location and drag to draw the AP element, using the horizontal and vertical rulers to place and size it.

2. If necessary, choose **Window→AP Elements** to display the **AP ELEMENTS** panel.
3. If necessary, in the **AP ELEMENTS** panel, double-click the AP element and type a name to rename the AP element.
4. Display the **CSS STYLES** panel in All mode.
5. Expand the **style** sub-tree and double-click the style that has the same name as the AP element.
6. In the **CSS Rule definition for <rule name>** dialog box, in the **Category** list box, select **Positioning.**
7. In the **Positioning** section, specify the values for positioning the AP element.

   > The positioning values of an AP element can also be set using the **Property Inspector.**

8. Click **Apply** to apply the changes to the AP element.
9. Click **OK.**
10. Position the insertion point within the AP element.
11. Insert content such as text, images, or a table into the AP element.
12. If necessary, apply a CSS style or attach an external style sheet.
13. If necessary, add more AP elements to the web page.

Positioning Properties of an AP Element

Dreamweaver allows you to display AP elements on a web page by setting their positioning properties. The properties can be set on the Property Inspector or in the CSS STYLES panel.

The table describes the positioning properties of an AP element.

Property	Specifies
Position	The positioning method of the AP element in the browser.
Visibility	How the AP element is initially displayed in the browser.
Width	The width of the AP element.
Z-Index	The stacking order of the AP element.
Height	The height of the AP element.
Overflow	How the AP element needs to display the content when the content exceeds the size of the element.
Placement	The location and size of the AP element with respect to the document window using the **Top, Right, Bottom,** and **Left** values.
Clip	The part of the content within the AP element that is visible using the **Top, Right, Bottom,** and **Left** values.

Procedure Reference: Modify the Stacking Order of an AP Element

To modify the stacking order of an AP element:

1. In the document window, select an AP element.
2. Set the stacking order.
   - In the **AP ELEMENTS** panel, drag an AP element to above or below another AP element.
   - Or, in the **Property Inspector,** in the **Z-Index** text box, specify the stacking number.

Procedure Reference: Set the Visibility of an AP Element

To set the visibility of an AP element:

1. Display the **AP ELEMENTS** panel.
2. Hide an AP element.
   - In the **AP ELEMENTS** panel, to the left of an AP element, in the eye icon column, click to hide the AP element.
   - In the **CSS STYLES** panel, specify the value for the `visibility` property as `hidden`.
3. If necessary, display an AP element.
   - To the left of an AP element, in the eye icon column, click the shut eye icon to display the AP element.
   - Specify the value for the `visibility` property as `visible`.
4. If necessary, click the eye icon at the top of the eye icon column to display or hide all AP elements on the web page simultaneously.

> When there is no eye icon, the visibility of the AP element is set to **Default,** and it inherits the visibility of its parent. If the AP element is not nested, the document body serves as its parent.

ACTIVITY 3-1
Creating AP Elements

Data Files:

upcomingevents.html

Before You Begin:

1. Delete the files and folders in the C:\084054Data\Our Global Company folder.
2. Copy the files and folders from the C:\084054Data\Working with AP Elements\Our Global Company folder to the C:\084054Data\Our Global Company folder.
3. From the C:\084054Data\Our Global Company folder, open the upcomingevents.txt file in Notepad.
4. From the **FILES** panel, open the upcomingevents.html file.

Scenario:

You need to add more information about each event displayed on the Upcoming Events page. However, you feel that adding more information to the page will lengthen the page and it will not be visually appealing. Therefore, you decide to add information so that it is unobtrusive.

What You Do	How You Do It
1. Create an AP element using the **Draw AP Div** button.	a. Choose **View→Rulers→Show** to enable rulers. b. Display the **INSERT** panel. c. In the **INSERT** panel, from the drop-down list, select **Layout** and then click **Draw AP Div.** d. In the document window, scroll down, click at the point of intersection of the 125 pixel mark on the horizontal ruler and the 340 pixel mark on the vertical ruler, and drag down and to the right to the point of intersection of the 535 pixel mark on the horizontal ruler and the 540 pixel mark on the vertical ruler. e. Display the **AP ELEMENTS** panel. f. In the **AP ELEMENTS** panel, double-click **apDiv1,** type *Aug15* and then press **Enter** to rename the AP element.
2. Insert the remaining AP elements.	a. In the document window, click between the links container and the left of the Aug15 AP element. b. Choose **Insert→Layout Objects→AP Div** to insert an AP element. c. In the **AP ELEMENTS** panel, double-click **apDiv1,** type *Sep02* and then press **Enter** to rename the AP element. d. Similarly, insert an AP element and rename it *Sep10*

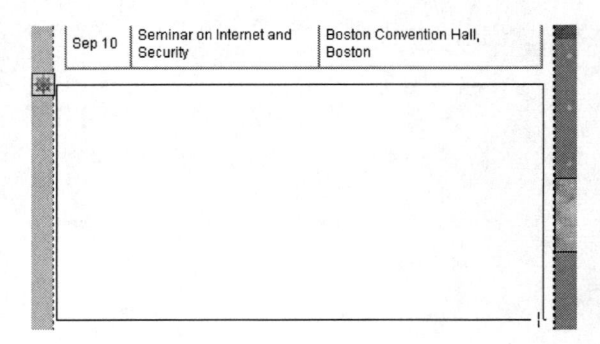

Adobe® Dreamweaver® CS4: Level 2

3. Specify the positioning properties for the first AP element.

    a. Double-click the **INSERT** panel to hide it.

    b. Display the **CSS STYLES** panel.

    c. In the **CSS STYLES** panel, in the **All Rules** section, scroll down to view the CSS rules in the **<style>** sub-tree.

    d. Observe that a CSS rule has been added for each of the AP elements.

```
─#main #text
─#main #images
─#Aug15
─#Sep02
─#Sep10
```

    e. Select **#Aug15** to display the properties for this rule.

    f. If necessary, in the **Properties for "#Aug15"** pane, in the text box to the right of the **height** property, type *200*

    g. If necessary, in the text box to the right of the **width** property, type *410*

    h. In the text box to the right of the **top** property, click and press **Delete** to remove the value for the top position, and then press **Enter.**

    i. In the text box to the right of the **left** property, click and press **Delete** to remove the value for the left position, and then press **Enter.**

    j. Click **Add Property,** and from the drop-down list, scroll down and select **margin-top.**

    k. In the text box to the right of the **margin-top** property, type *10* and press **Enter.**

Lesson 3: Working with AP Elements   **69**

Adobe® Dreamweaver® CS4: Level 2

4.	Position the other AP elements.	a.	In the **All Rules** section, select **#Sep02**.
		b.	In the **Properties for "#Sep02"** pane, in the text box to the right of the **height** property, type *200* and press **Enter**.
		c.	In the text box to the right of the **width** property, type *410* and press **Enter**.
		d.	Click **Add Property,** and in the drop-down list, scroll down and select **margin-top**.
		e.	In the text box to the right of the **margin-top** property, type *10* and press **Enter**.
		f.	Similarly, for the Sep10 AP element, change the **height** and **width** values to *200* and *410* respectively, and add the **margin-top** property with the value *10*
5.	Add a background color for the AP elements.	a.	In the **CSS STYLES** panel, in the **All Rules** section, select **#Aug15**.
		b.	In the **Properties for "#Aug15"** pane, click **Add Property,** and from the drop-down list, select **background-color**.
		c.	In the text box to the right of the **background-color** property, type *#EEE* and press **Enter**.
		d.	Similarly, for the Sep02 and Sep10 AP elements, add the **background-color** with the values *#DDD* and *#CCC* respectively.
6.	Move the Aug15 AP element to within the `div` tag.	a.	Select the **AP ELEMENTS** tab, and in the panel, select the **Aug15** AP element.
		b.	Switch to Code view.
		c.	In line 60, observe that the tag for the Aug15 AP element is selected.
		d.	Choose **Edit→Cut**.
		e.	In the document window, scroll down, click at the end of line 106, and press **Enter**.
		f.	Choose **Edit→Paste**.
		g.	Switch to Design view.

Lesson 3: Working with AP Elements

7.	Add content to the AP elements.	a.	Switch to Notepad.
		b.	Choose **Format→Word Wrap** to wrap the text.
		c.	In the first line, click before the text "Six Sigma Workshop", hold down **Shift,** and in the seventh line of text, click after the text "Workshop materials will be provided for participants."
		d.	Choose **Edit→Copy.**
		e.	Switch to Dreamweaver.
		f.	In the document window, scroll down, and in the **AP ELEMENTS** panel, select the **Aug15** AP element.
		g.	In Design view, click in the selected AP element, and choose **Edit→Paste** to place the text into the AP element.
		h.	In the Aug15 AP element, select the text.
		i.	In the **Property Inspector,** from the **Class** drop-down list, select **aptext** to apply the class style to the selected text.
		j.	Similarly, copy the event information for the National Convention of Project Consultants and the Seminar on Internet and Security events, and paste it in the Sep02 and Sep10 AP elements, respectively, and apply the aptext class style.
8.	Preview the page in a browser.	a.	Close the Notepad file.
		b.	Save the upcomingevents.html file.
		c.	Preview the page in Internet Explorer.
		d.	Observe that the last inserted AP element, which contains information on the Seminar on Internet and Security event, is visible.
		e.	Close the Internet Explorer window.
9.	Set the visibility of the AP elements.	a.	In the **AP ELEMENTS** panel, to the left of the Sep10 AP element, click in the eye icon column.

Lesson 3: Working with AP Elements

b. In the eye icon column, to the left of the Sep10 AP element, observe that a shut-eye icon is displayed and, in the document window, observe that the Sep10 AP element is hidden.

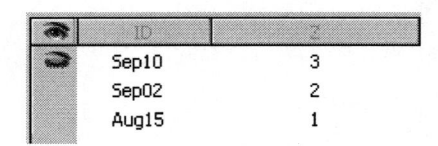

ID	Z
Sep10	3
Sep02	2
Aug15	1

c. To the left of the Sep02 AP element, click in the eye icon column to hide it.

d. To the left of the Aug15 AP element, click in the eye icon column to hide it.

10. Preview the upcoming events page in a browser.

a. Save the upcomingevents.html file.

b. Preview the web page in Internet Explorer.

c. Observe that the information on AP elements is not displayed.

d. Close the Internet Explorer window.

TOPIC B
Control AP Elements

You created AP elements and modified their properties. You may now want to vary their appearance at runtime. In this topic, you will dynamically control AP elements.

When developing complex web pages, you may need to dynamically vary the display of certain elements. Displaying information based on user interaction will evoke user interest and enhance the visual appeal of the website. You can achieve this by applying behaviors to AP elements.

Behavior

A *behavior* is a combination of an event and an action triggered by the event. Using the **Behaviors** tab in the **TAG INSPECTOR** panel, you can define behaviors for elements on a page. The behaviors applied allow the user to interact with the element on the web page.

The Behaviors Tab

The **Behaviors** tab, available in the **TAG INSPECTOR** panel, is used to create and add new behaviors or alter certain parameters of behaviors that were created. Several options are available within the **Behaviors** tab.

Option	Description
Show set events	Displays events that have been assigned to a particular page element.
Show all events	Displays, in alphabetical order, all default events that are supported by a given element.
Add behavior	Displays a set of behaviors that can be assigned to elements in a document.
Remove event	Deletes the selected event from the **Behaviors** tab.
Move event value up	Moves the selected element upward in the list of events.
Move event value down	Moves the selected element downward in the list of events.

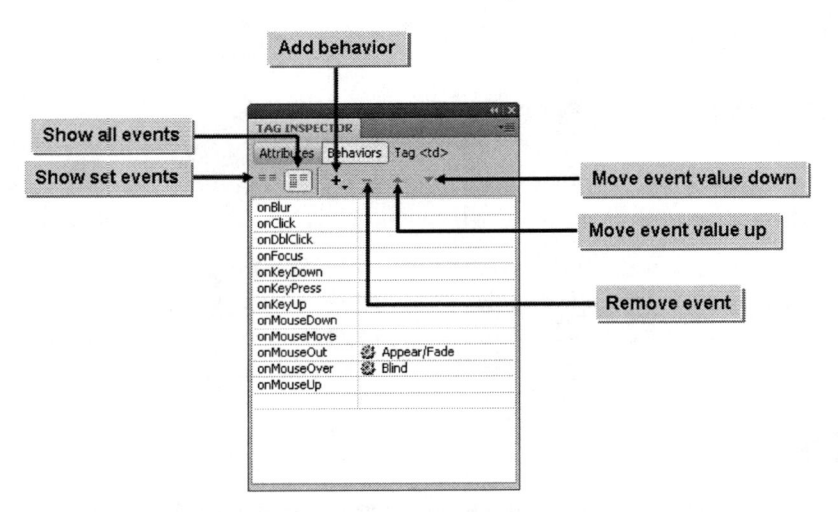

Figure 3-3: The TAG INSPECTOR panel displaying the Behaviors tab.

Built-in Behaviors

The table lists the different behaviors provided by Adobe Dreamweaver.

Behavior	Description
Call JavaScript	Calls a custom JavaScript function when an event occurs.
Change Property	Changes the value of an object's properties such as the background color of div or the action of a form.
Check Plugin	Checks the plug-in installed on visitors' systems and redirects them to different pages based on the plug-in.
Drag AP Element	Allows visitors to drag a positioned AP element. This behavior is mainly used in puzzles, slider controls, and movable interface elements.
Effects	Adds a visual effect to an object.
Go To URL	Opens a new page in the current window when a link is clicked.
Jump Menu	Allows users to select a web page from the menu and navigate to it. This behavior is automatically applied when a **Jump** menu is created.
Jump Menu Go	Adds a **Go** button to the **Jump** menu so that the behavior is triggered when users click the button.
Open Browser Window	Opens a web page in a new window upon clicking a link.

Behavior	Description
Pop-up Message	Displays a JavaScript alert with the message specified by the developer. JavaScript alerts have only one button, the **OK** button, so this behavior is used to give user information rather than present a choice.
Preload Images	Shortens the display time of an image by caching images that are not displayed when the page is initially loaded.
Set Nav Bar Image	Modifies an image into a navigation bar image.
Set Text	Sets text or replaces the original content with new content or formatting. Text can be set for containers, frames, status bars, and text fields.
Show-Hide Elements	Shows, hides, or restores the default visibility of an element.
Swap Image	Substitutes one image with another and produces a rollover effect.
Swap Image Restore	Restores the original image in place of the swapped image. It is automatically triggered when the swap image behavior is applied.
Validate Form	Checks the content input in a form. This ensures that the user has entered the correct type of data.

The Show Events For Command

The **Show Events For** command, available on the **Add Behavior** menu, allows you to display events that are specific to a browser or HTML version on the **Behaviors** tab.

Behavior Events

The table describes the different events that are available for most browsers to trigger behaviors.

Event	Triggers Behavior When Users
`onBlur`	Select a specified item on the page and then move the focus away from the item.
`onClick`	Click in a specified location on the page.
`onDblClick`	Double-click in a specified location on the page.
`onFocus`	Select a specified item on the page.
`onKeyDown`	Continue to hold down a key after pressing it.
`onKeyPress`	Press a key.
`onKeyUp`	Release a key after pressing it.
`onMouseDown`	Press the left mouse button on a specified location on the page.

Event	Triggers Behavior When Users
onMouseMove	Move the mouse pointer.
onMouseOut	Move the mouse pointer away from a specified location on the page.
onMouseOver	Position the mouse pointer over a specified location on the page.
onMouseUp	Release the mouse button.

Behavior Effects

Behavior effects are used to display web page elements with visual effects upon a certain behavior. Predefined effects are available in Dreamweaver that can be added to elements to create dynamic web pages.

The table describes the predefined effects.

Effect	Description
Appear/Fade	The element appears on or fades off the web page.
Blind	The element is displayed with a visual effect of a window blind scrolling up or down.
Grow/Shrink	The element increases or decreases in size.
Highlight	The element is highlighted with a change in appearance, such as change of text color.
Shake	The element shakes from side to side.
Slide	The element slides up or down.
Squish	The element reduces in size and disappears. The upper-left corner is the anchor point for the effect.

How to Control AP Elements

Procedure Reference: Apply a Behavior Effect to an Element

To apply a behavior effect to an element:

1. In the document window, select the element for which the behavior effect is to be added.
2. If necessary, in the **TAG INSPECTOR** panel, click **Behaviors** to display behavior options.
3. If necessary, click the **Show all events** button to display the events available for the selected element.
4. Click the **Add behavior** button, choose **Effects,** and then choose the effect type.
5. In the **<Effect>** dialog box, specify the parameters for the effect.
6. Click **OK** to create the effect for the element.
7. If necessary, click the **Show set events** button to display the effects applied to the selected element.
8. If necessary, click the event, and from the drop-down list, select an event to specify the event action.
9. If necessary, add more behavior effects.
10. If necessary, select an event and click the **Remove event** button to delete an event and its effect.
11. Save the changes to the web page and preview it in the browser.

ACTIVITY 3-2
Controlling the Visibility of AP Elements Dynamically

Data Files:

upcomingevents.html

Before You Begin:

The upcomingevents.html file is open.

Scenario:

You have the information for each event in an AP element. However, you want to display this information only upon user interaction. You want to enhance the user experience by displaying this information with a visual effect when the user moves the mouse pointer near to the event name and hide the information when the mouse pointer is moved away from it.

What You Do	How You Do It
1. Add a behavior effect to display an AP element.	a. Choose **Window→Behaviors** to display the **Behaviors** tab in the **TAG INSPECTOR** panel. b. In the document window, in the second row of the table, select the text **"Six Sigma Workshop"**. c. In the **TAG INSPECTOR** panel, click the **Add behavior** button, and choose **Effects→Blind**. d. In the **Blind** dialog box, from the **Target Element** drop-down list, select **div "Aug15"**. e. From the **Effect** drop-down list, select **Blind down** and click **OK**. f. In the **TAG INSPECTOR** panel, click the **Show all events** button, to display all of the events. g. In the **TAG INSPECTOR** panel, click the **Show set events** button, to display only the events for which behaviors are applied. h. Click **onClick,** and from the drop-down list, select **onMouseOver** to set the behavior to take place only when the mouse pointer is moved over the text "Six Sigma Workshop". i. If necessary, to the right of **onClick,** click **Blind,** and click the **Remove event** button. *Remove the event only if a duplicate entry is created when the effect is added.*

j. In the third row of the table, select the text **"National Convention of Project Consultants",** create a **Blind** effect, with the **Target Element** as **div "Sep02"** and the **Effect** as **Blind down,** and then assign the effect to the **onMouseOver** event.

k. In the last row of the table, select the text **"Seminar on Internet and Security",** create a **Blind** effect, with the **Target Element** as **div "Sep10"** and the **Effect** as **Blind down,** and then assign the effect to the **onMouseOver** event.

2. Add a behavior effect to hide the AP element.

    a. In the document window, in the second row of the table, select the text **"Six Sigma Workshop"**.

    b. In the **TAG INSPECTOR** panel, click the **Add behavior** button and choose **Effects→Blind**.

    c. In the **Blind** dialog box, from the **Target Element** drop-down list, select **div "Aug15"**.

    d. In the **Effect** drop-down list, verify that **Blind up** is selected and click **OK**.

    e. In the **TAG INSPECTOR** panel, observe that the **Blind** effect is assigned to the **onClick** event.

    f. Click **onClick,** and from the drop-down list, select **onMouseOut** to set the behavior to take place when the mouse pointer is moved away from the text "Six Sigma Workshop".

    g. If necessary, to the right of **onClick,** click **Blind** and then click the **Remove event** button.

    h. In the third row of the table, select the text **"National Convention of Project Consultants"**, add a **Blind** effect, set the **Target Element** as **div "Sep02"** and the **Effect** as **Blind up,** and then assign the effect to the **onMouseOut** event.

    i. In the last row of the table, select the text **"Seminar on Internet and Security"**, add a **Blind** effect, set the **Target Element** as **div "Sep10"** and the **Effect** as **Blind up,** and then assign the effect to the **onMouseOut** event.

3. Preview the web page in a browser.

a. Save the upcomingevents.html file.

b. In the **Copy Dependent Files** message box, click **OK.**

c. Preview the web page in Internet Explorer.

d. Move the mouse pointer over the text "Six Sigma Workshop" to view the event information with a blind effect, and then move the mouse pointer away from the text "Six Sigma Workshop" to hide the information.

e. Close the Internet Explorer window.

f. Close the upcomingevents.html file.

Lesson 3 Follow-up

In this lesson, you created and controlled AP elements. Manipulating AP elements enables you to accurately position elements on a web page and dynamically control them.

1. **When would you use AP elements on your web page? Why?**

2. **What behavior effects might you add to AP elements to enhance the display of page elements? Why?**

4 Working with Spry Elements

Lesson Time: 1 hour(s), 20 minutes

Lesson Objectives:

In this lesson, you will work with Spry elements.

You will:

- Use Spry interface widgets.
- Modify Spry widgets.
- Use Spry data set.

Introduction

You used AP elements to enhance the presentation of content on your web pages. Now, you may need to use advanced interface and data objects to improve users' experiences. In this lesson, you will use Spry elements.

Presenting extensive content on a web page is a challenging task. Displaying it without cluttering the page will raise user interest in your site. Dreamweaver's Spry framework provides you with elements that allow you to build advanced user interface components, and organize data effectively.

TOPIC A
Use Spry Interface Widgets

You used AP elements to display information dynamically on user interaction. Now, you may need to add advanced user interface elements such as panels, menus, or tabs. In this topic, you will use the Spry user interface widgets.

A common problem faced by web designers is the lack of space to display all content. This may result in content being spread across many pages resulting in larger websites. Using Spry interface widgets, you can present content effectively in different formats and layouts.

Spry User Interface Widgets

Spry user interface widgets are elements that enable user interaction on a web page. There are five user interface widgets available. The following table lists the five widgets and their behavior.

Widget	Used to
Spry Menu Bar	Create a set of menu buttons. Submenus are displayed as drop-down lists when the user clicks one of the menu buttons.
Spry Tabbed Panels	Create a panel containing many tabs. Users can view the content of a tab by selecting it.
Spry Collapsible Panel	Create a single panel that can contain a large amount of content. Users can click the panel to hide or view the content.
Spry Accordion	Create a set of collapsible panels that can be used to store a large amount of content in a small space. Users can hide or view the content by selecting a tab.
Spry Tooltip	Create a tooltip to display text or images in a tooltip for text or any page element. Users can move the mouse pointer over the element to view the information.

Spry Widget

A Spry widget consists of three parts: the widget structure, behavior, and styling. The widget structure is an HTML code block that states the structural composition of the widget. The widget behavior is a JavaScript code block that controls the widget's response to user-initiated events. The widget styling is a CSS code block that defines the appearance of the widget.

How to Use Spry Interface Widgets

Procedure Reference: Insert a Spry Menu Bar

To insert a Spry menu bar:

1. Position the insertion point where the menu bar is to be inserted.
2. Display the **Spry Menu Bar** dialog box.
   - Choose **Insert→Layout Objects→Spry Menu Bar.**
   - Choose **Insert→Spry→Spry Menu Bar.**
   - In the **INSERT** panel, from the drop-down list, select **Layout,** and click **Spry Menu Bar.**
   - Or, in the **INSERT** panel, from the drop-down list, select **Spry,** and click **Spry Menu Bar.**
3. In the **Spry Menu Bar** dialog box, select **Horizontal** or **Vertical** and click **OK** to insert the Spry menu bar.
4. In the **Property Inspector,** in the **Menu Bar** text box, type a name for the menu bar.
5. If necessary, above the first list box, click the **Add menu item** button to add a menu item.
6. If necessary, above the second list box, click the **Add menu item** button to add a submenu item for the corresponding main menu item.
7. Select a menu item, and in the **Text** text box, type a name for the menu item.
8. Create a link for a menu item.
   a. In either of the list boxes, select the menu item for which the link has to be created.
   b. In the **Link** text box, type the name of the web page you want to link to, or next to the **Link** text box, click the **Browse** button, navigate to and select the web page you want to link to, and click **OK.**
9. In the **Title** text box, type a title.
10. If necessary, in the **Target** text box, type a target for the menu item.
11. If necessary, select a menu item and click the **Move item up** or **Move item down** button to change the position of the menu item on the menu bar.
12. If necessary, select a menu item and click the **Remove menu item** button to remove the menu item.
13. Save the web page.
14. In the **Copy Dependent Files** message box, click **OK.**
15. Preview the page in a browser.

Procedure Reference: Create Spry Tabbed Panels

To create Spry tabbed panels:

1. Position the insertion point where the tabbed panel is to be inserted.

2. Insert the Spry tabbed panels.
   - Choose **Insert→Layout Objects→Spry Tabbed Panels.**
   - Choose **Insert→Spry→Spry Tabbed Panels.**
   - In the **INSERT** panel, from the drop-down list, select **Layout,** and click **Spry Tabbed Panels.**
   - Or, in the **INSERT** panel, from the drop-down list, select **Spry,** and click **Spry Tabbed Panels.**
3. In the **Property Inspector,** in the **Tabbed panels** text box, type a name for the tabbed panel.

> By default, two tabs are inserted.

4. If necessary, above the **Panels** list box, click the **Add panel** button to add more tabs.
5. Add content on the tabs.
   a. Select the tab.
      - In the document window, click the eye icon on a tab to display its content.
      - Or, in the **Property Inspector,** in the **Panels** list box, select a tab.
   b. Delete the default tab heading and type a heading for the tab.
   c. Delete the default content and type the required content.
6. If necessary, select a tab and format it using the **Property Inspector.**
7. If necessary, select a tab, and in the **Property Inspector,** click the **Remove panel** button to remove a tab.
8. Save the web page.
9. In the **Copy Dependent Files** message box, click **OK.**
10. Preview the page in a browser.

Procedure Reference: Insert a Spry Accordion Panel

To insert a Spry accordion panel:
1. Position the insertion point where the accordion panel is to be inserted.
2. Insert the Spry accordion panel.
   - Choose **Insert→Layout Objects→Spry Accordion.**
   - Choose **Insert→Spry→Spry Accordion.**
   - In the **INSERT** panel, from the drop-down list, select **Layout,** and click **Spry Accordion.**
   - Or, in the **INSERT** panel, from the drop-down list, select **Spry,** and click **Spry Accordion.**
3. In the **Property Inspector,** in the **Accordion** text box, type a name for the accordion panel.
4. If necessary, above the **Panels** list box, click the **Add panel** button to add a panel.
5. Add content in the panels.
   a. Select the panel.

- In the document window, click the eye icon on a panel label to display its content.
- Or, in the **Property Inspector,** in the **Panels** list box, select a panel.
  b. Delete the default panel heading and type a heading for the panel.
  c. Delete the default content and type the required content.
6. If necessary, in the **Panels** list box, select a panel and click the **Move panel up in list** or **Move panel down in list** button to change the position of the panel.
7. If necessary, in the **Panels** list box, select a panel and click the **Remove panel** button to remove it.
8. Save the web page.
9. In the **Copy Dependent Files** message box, click **OK.**
10. Preview the page in a browser.

Procedure Reference: Insert a Spry Collapsible Panel

To insert a Spry collapsible panel:
1. Position the insertion point where the collapsible panel is to be inserted.
2. Insert the Spry collapsible panel.
   - Choose **Insert→Layout Objects→Spry Collapsible Panel.**
   - Choose **Insert→Spry→Spry Collapsible Panel.**
   - In the **INSERT** panel, from the drop-down list, select **Layout,** and click **Spry Collapsible Panel.**
   - Or, in the **INSERT** panel, from the drop-down list, select **Spry,** and click **Spry Collapsible Panel.**
3. In the **Property Inspector,** in the **Collapsible panel** text box, type a name for the panel.
4. From the **Display** drop-down list, select an option.
   - Select **Closed** to display a minimized panel on the web page.
   - Select **Open** to display the contents of the panel on the web page.
5. From the **Default state** drop-down list, select a default display option.
6. If necessary, uncheck the **Enable animation** check box.

> Checking the **Enable animation** check box will animate the collapsing of the panel when viewed in a browser.

7. Select a panel.
8. Modify the panel content.
   - Delete the default panel heading and type a heading for the panel.
   - Delete the default content and type the required content.
9. Save the web page.
10. In the **Copy Dependent Files** message box, click **OK.**
11. Preview the page in a browser.

Procedure Reference: Insert a Spry Tooltip

To insert a Spry tooltip:

1. Select the element for which you want the tooltip to be displayed.
2. Insert the Spry tooltip.
   - Choose **Insert→Spry→Spry Tooltip.**
   - Or, in the **INSERT** panel, from the drop-down list, select **Spry,** and click **Spry Tooltip.**
3. In the document window, scroll to the bottom of the page, and delete the default content for the tooltip.
4. Add content such as text or images to be displayed as a tooltip.
5. In the **Property Inspector,** in the **Spry Tooltip** text box, type a name for the tooltip.
6. From the **Trigger** drop-down list, select the page element that activates the tooltip.
7. If necessary, check the **Follow Mouse** check box to allow the tooltip to follow the mouse pointer when the mouse pointer moves over the selected page element.
8. If necessary, check the **Hide on Mouse Out** check box to hide the tooltip when the mouse pointer is moved away from the selected page element but display it as long as it hovers over the tooltip.
9. If necessary, in the **Horizontal offset** text box, type a value in pixels to specify the horizontal distance between the tootip and the mouse pointer.
10. If necessary, in the **Vertical offset** text box, type a value in pixels to specify the vertical distance between the tootip and the mouse pointer.
11. In the **Show delay** text box, type a value in milliseconds to specify the delay after which the tooltip appears.
12. In the **Hide delay** text box, type a value in milliseconds to specify the delay after which the tooltip disappears.
13. In the **Effect** section, select an effect.
    - Select **None** if no effect is required when the tooltip appears.
    - Select **Blind** if an effect similar to a window blind opening or closing is required when the tooltip appears and disappears.
    - Select **Fade** if a fading in and fading out effect is required when the tooltip appears and disappears.
14. Save the web page.
15. In the **Copy Dependent Files** message box, click **OK.**
16. Preview the page in a browser.

ACTIVITY 4-1
Inserting a Spry Tabbed Panel

Data Files:

clients.html

Before You Begin:
1. From the **FILES** panel, open the clients.html file.
2. Close the **Design Notes** dialog box.

Scenario:
You feel that separating the clients list from the partners list on the Clients and Partners page will make the information easy to read. While presenting the content separately, you also want to make it more appealing for site visitors.

What You Do	How You Do It
1. Insert a Spry tabbed panel.	a. In the document window, click after the heading "Clients and Partners" and press **Enter**.
	b. Display the **INSERT** panel.
	c. In the **INSERT** panel, click **Spry Tabbed Panels**.
	d. In the document window, in the **Spry Tabbed Panels: TabbedPanels1** tabbed panel, on the **Tab1** tab, select the text "**Tab 1**", and type *Clients*
	e. On the **Tab2** tab, select the text "**Tab 2**", and type *Partners*

Lesson 4: Working with Spry Elements

2. Add content to the tabs.

   a. Below the tabbed panel, click before the text "Through multitudes", hold down **Shift,** and click after the text "6. IBooks Publishing Company".

   b. Choose **Edit→Cut.**

   c. On the **Clients** tab, select the text **"Content 1".**

   d. Choose **Edit→Paste.**

   e. In the document window, scroll down, click before the text "To help clients", hold down **Shift,** and click after the text "e-Knowledge Inc."

   f. Choose **Edit→Cut.**

   g. Scroll up, and on the **Partners** tab, click the **Click to show panel content** icon.

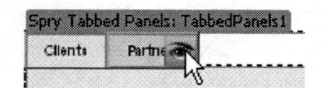

   h. Select the text **"Content 2".**

   i. Choose **Edit→Paste.**

   j. Below the tabbed panel, click before the text "Clients", scroll down, hold down **Shift,** and click after the text "Partners".

   k. Press **Delete.**

3.	Modify the background color of the tabs.	a.	Display the **CSS STYLES** panel.
		b.	In the document window, scroll up, and on the **Clients** tab, click the **Click to show panel content** icon.
		c.	On the status bar, in the tag selector, verify that **<li.TabbedPanelsTab>** is selected.
		d.	In the **CSS STYLES** panel, click **Current,** and click the **Edit Rule** button.
		e.	In the **CSS Rule Definition for .TabbedPanelsTabSelected in SpryTabbedPanels.css** dialog box, in the **Category** list box, select **Background.**
		f.	In the **Background-color** text box, double-click and type *#9AD6EF*
		g.	Click **OK.**
4.	Modify the background color of the tabbed panel content region.	a.	In the tabbed panel, on the **Clients** tab, click before the text "Through multitudes of projects".
		b.	On the status bar, in the tag selector, select **<div.TabbedPanelsContentGroup>.**
		c.	In the **CSS STYLES** panel, click the **Edit Rule** button.
		d.	In the **CSS Rule Definition for .TabbedPanelsContentGroup in SpryTabbedPanels.css** dialog box, in the **Background-color** text box, double-click and type *#B4D6EF*
		e.	Click **OK.**

5. Preview the web page in a browser.
   a. Save all the open files.
   b. In the **Copy Dependent Files** message box, click **OK.**
   c. Preview the web page in Internet Explorer.
   d. Select the **Partners** tab to view the content.
   e. Select the **Clients** tab to view the content.
   f. Close the Internet Explorer window.
   g. Close the clients.html file.

Adobe® Dreamweaver® CS4: Level 2

ACTIVITY 4-2
Inserting Spry Tooltips

Data Files:

newproducts.html

Before You Begin:

From the **FILES** panel, open the newproducts.html file.

Scenario:

The Product Manager has provided you some additional information about the new products developed. This information can be selectively displayed for each product. You feel that this information should be presented more attractively when the user hovers over each product.

What You Do	How You Do It
1. Add a Spry tooltip to the first image.	a. In the document window, in the second row of the table, in the second cell, click the image to select it.
	b. In the **INSERT** panel, from the drop-down list, select **Spry**.
	c. Scroll down to the bottom of the panel, and click **Spry Tooltip**.
	d. Scroll to the bottom of the document window.
	e. Observe that a Spry Tooltip element is added displaying the content "Tooltip content goes here."
	f. In the Spry Tooltip element, select the text "Tooltip content goes here."
	g. Type the text *This tool allows individuals and organizations to store and share contact information. The free trial works for 30 days. Rating:*

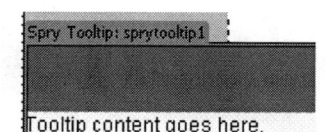

Lesson 4: Working with Spry Elements   95

2. Add an image to the tooltip.
   a. Choose **Insert→Image**.
   b. In the **Select Image Source** dialog box, navigate to the C:\084054Data\OurGlobal company\images folder.
   c. Select the 3star.png image and click **OK**.
   d. In the **Image Tag Accessibility Attributes** dialog box, in the **Alternate text** text box, type *Three Star* and click **OK**.

3. Specify the properties for the tooltip.
   a. In the document window, select **Spry Tooltip: sprytooltip1**.
   b. In the **Property Inspector,** check the **Follow mouse** check box to specify that the tooltip should follow the mouse pointer.
   c. Check the **Hide on mouse out** check box.
   d. In the **Show delay** text box, click and type *100*
   e. In the **Hide delay** text box, click and type *100*
   f. In the **Effect** section, select **Fade**.

4. Add Spry tooltips for other images.

   a. In the document window, scroll up, and in the second row of the table, in the third cell, click the image to select it.

   b. In the **INSERT** panel, click **Spry Tooltip.**

   c. In the document window, scroll down, and in the **Spry Tooltip: sprytooltip2** tooltip element, select the default tooltip content, and type the text *This software offers features to customize all your employee related HR requirements. The free trial works for 30 days. Rating:*

   d. Add the image 4star.png with the alternate text *Four Star*

   e. In the document window, select **Spry Tooltip: sprytooltip2,** and in the **Property Inspector,** check the **Follow mouse** and **Hide on mouse out** check boxes.

   f. Set the values for **Show delay** to *100* and **Hide delay** to *100* and **Effect** to **Fade.**

   g. Similarly, add a tooltip for the last image, with the tooltip content *This utility allows individuals to schedule meetings, events, and appointments. The free trial works for 30 days. Rating:* and insert the 5star.png image with the alternate text *Five Star*

   h. Check the **Follow mouse** and **Hide on mouse out** check boxes.

   i. Set the tooltip properties **Show delay** to *100* and **Hide delay** to *100* and **Effect** to **Fade.**

5. Preview the web page in a browser.

   a. Save the newproducts.html file.

   b. In the **Copy Dependent Files** message box, click **OK.**

   c. Preview the web page in Internet Explorer.

   d. Move the mouse pointer over the image for **OGC Contact Manager 1.0** to view the tooltip.

   e. Close the Internet Explorer window.

TOPIC B
Modify Spry Widgets

You added Spry widgets to your web pages. You may now want to enhance their appearance on the pages. In this topic, you will modify Spry widgets.

Often, when using Spry elements on your web pages, you need to change their properties and appearance to suit the theme of the website. Modifying the Spry widgets will help you alter their appearance and blend with other elements on your pages.

How to Modify Spry Widgets
Procedure Reference: Modify a Spry Widget

To modify a Spry widget:

1. In the **CSS STYLES** panel, expand the sub-tree of the external style sheet of a Spry widget.
2. Select a CSS rule to be modified.
3. Click the **Edit Rule** button to display the **CSS Rule Definition** dialog box for the selected rule.
4. Specify the CSS properties to modify the Spry widget.
5. Click **OK** to confirm the properties.
6. Save all the files.
7. Preview the page in a browser.

ACTIVITY 4-3
Modifying a Spry Widget on a Web Page

Data Files:

newproducts.html

Before You Begin:

The newproducts.html file is open.

Scenario:

Your colleagues appreciate the tooltips you inserted for the images on the New Products page. However, you feel that the tooltips need to blend better with the page colors.

What You Do	How You Do It
1. Access CSS properties for the Spry tooltips.	a. In the **CSS STYLES** panel, click **All**. b. In the **All Rules** section, collapse the **ogc_styles.css** sub-tree, and expand the **SpryTooltip.css** sub-tree. c. Select **.tooltipContent,** and at the bottom of the panel, click the **Edit Rule** button.
2. Modify CSS properties for the tooltips.	a. In the **Background-color** text box, double-click and type *#DFFFFF* b. In the **Category** list box, select **Type**. c. From the **Font-family** drop-down list, select **Arial, Helvetica, sans-serif**. d. From the **Font-size** drop-down list, select **10**. e. In the **Category** list box, select **Box**. f. In the **Width** text box, type *175* g. In the **Height** text box, type *70* h. In the **Padding** section, in the **Top** text box, type *5*

Lesson 4: Working with Spry Elements   99

Adobe® Dreamweaver® CS4: Level 2

3.	Add CSS properties to define a border for the tooltips.	a.	In the **Category** list box, select **Border**.
		b.	In the **Style** section, verify that the **Same for all** check box is checked, and from the **Top** drop-down list, select **solid.**
		c.	In the **Width** section, verify that the **Same for all** check box is checked, and from the **Top** drop-down list, select **thin.**
		d.	In the **Color** section, verify that the **Same for all** check box is checked, and in the **Top** text box, click and type *#036*
		e.	Click **OK.**
4.	Preview the web page in a browser.	a.	Save all the open files.
		b.	Preview the web page in Internet Explorer.
		c.	Move the mouse pointer over the image for **OGC Contact Manager 1.0** to view the tooltip.
		d.	Close the Internet Explorer window.
		e.	Close the newproducts.html file.

TOPIC C
Use Spry Data Sets

You used Spry widgets to present content. Now, you may need to integrate an external data source into the web page. In this topic, you will display content on your pages using Spry data sets.

You may already have data in an external data source such as XML or an HTML table that you want to display on your page. Re-creating such data on a web page could be tedious and time-consuming. Instead, you can integrate the external data source on the web page so that the data can be updated dynamically. By using Spry data sets, you can dynamically display data from an external XML or HTML file, which can be frequently updated.

XML

Definition:
eXtensible Markup Language or *XML* is a programming language that is used to describe the structure of data in a document. The tags used to describe data are not predefined; they are defined by the developer. XML can be used to generate different formats of the same file. Designers can have just one XML document and update it to reflect changes in other formats of the document.

Example:

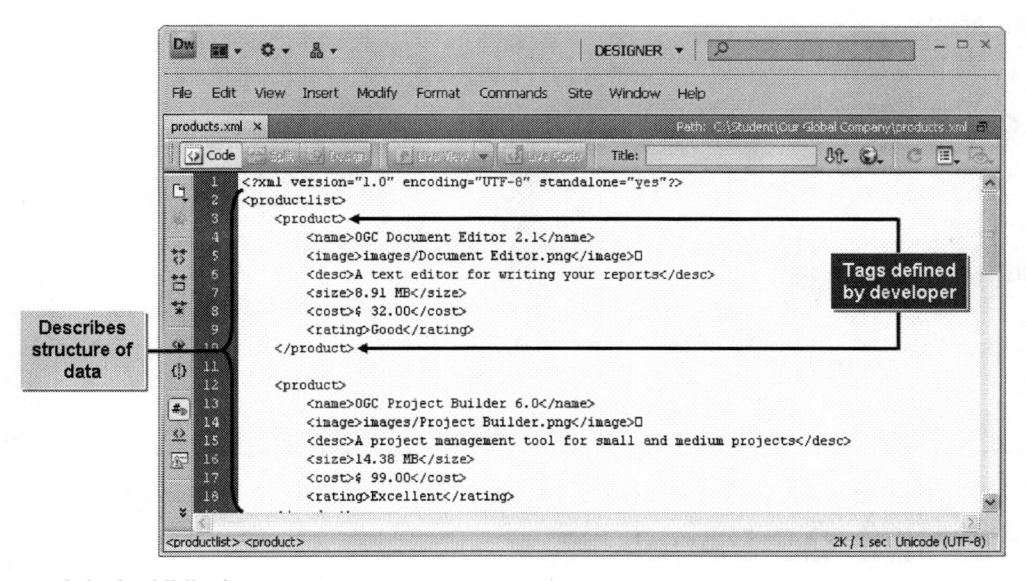

Figure 4-1: An XML document.

Spry XML Data Set

A *Spry XML data set* is a tool provided by Dreamweaver to display XML data on a web page. When users open a web page in a browser, the data set loads an array of XML data. Developers can interact with the data set object to dynamically display content on the web page. An advantage of the Spry XML data set is that updating data in the XML file will automatically reflect on the web page.

Document Type Definition (DTD)

Document Type Definition (DTD) is a language used for describing an XML schema. It uses a set of declarations that conform to the XML markup syntax, and describes the type of document in terms of its structure. It is also used to declare constructs that may be required to interpret XML documents.

Spry HTML Data Set

A *Spry HTML data set* is used to display data on web pages from standard HTML tables or other structured HTML elements. It allows you to choose the data container and select data to be displayed. Data can be selectively displayed using various predefined layouts. Spry HTML data sets are used when small amounts of data are to be displayed and managed.

Spry Data Set Controls

In addition to the Spry XML and HTML data sets, there are three other data objects that help present dynamic data. Using these, you can insert and display data on your pages and enhance user interaction.

Data Object	Description
Spry Region	Wraps around data objects such as tables and repeat lists. All Spry data objects must be enclosed within a Spry region.
Spry Repeat	Adds repeating regions to display data. It allows you to format and add data as needed.
Spry Repeat List	Displays data as lists. Data can be presented as an ordered list, an unordered list, a definition list, or a drop-down list.

The BINDINGS Panel

The **BINDINGS** panel is used to define and edit dynamic sources of content, such as XML, for a web page. It allows you to perform various tasks such as adding dynamic content to the page and modifying content sources.

Figure 4-2: XML schema displayed in the BINDINGS panel.

Live View

Live view enables you to view your web page in Dreamweaver as it would appear in a browser. It is a quick way to preview dynamic data and user interaction on web pages. While previewing a page in Live view, you cannot edit the content of the page. However, you can modify it in Code view, and changes can be previewed in Live view instantly. You can also freeze JavaScript to check its current state and disable JavaScript and plug-ins to check how the page will display in a browser without JavaScript and plug-ins.

How to Use Spry Data Set

Procedure Reference: Insert a Spry XML Data Set

To insert a Spry XML data set:

1. Open an HTML file and place the insertion point where you want to insert the XML data set.
2. Display the **Spry Data Set** wizard.
   - Choose **Insert→Spry→Spry Data Set.**
   - In the **BINDINGS** panel, click the Plus button (+), and choose **Spry Data Set.**
   - Or, in the **INSERT** panel, from the drop-down list, select **Spry** and click **Spry Data Set.**
3. From the **Select Data Type** drop-down list, select **XML.**
4. In the **Data Set Name** text box, type a name for the data set.
5. Next to the **Specify Data File** text box, click **Browse,** navigate to and select an XML file that contains the data, and click **OK.**
6. If necessary, in the **Row element** list box, select an element to display the location of the element in the **XPath** text box and a preview of the data set in the **Data Preview** section.
7. Click **Next.**

8. If necessary, in the **Set Data Options** section, select a column.
   - In the **Data Preview** section, click the heading of a column.
   - Click the **Select next column** button to select the column on the right of the current column.
   - Click the **Select previous column** button to select the column on the left of the current column.
   - From the **Column Name** drop-down list, select a column.
9. If necessary, from the **Type** drop-down list, select a data type for the selected column.
10. If necessary, set the data options.
    - From the **Sort Column** drop-down list, select a column to sort the data set and from the drop-down list to the right of the **Sort Column** drop-down list, select the direction you want to use to sort the data set.
    - Check the **Filter out duplicate rows** check box to avoid displaying duplicate rows of data.
    - Check the **Disable Data caching** check box to avoid creating a cache of the data and use the current data in the data set.
    - Check the **Autorefresh Data** check box, and in the text box to the right, specify the time in milliseconds to refresh the data at the specified interval.
11. Click **Next.**
12. In the **Choose Insert Options** section, select a display option.
    - Select **Insert table** to insert HTML code for displaying the data as a Spry table.
    - Select **Insert master/detail layout** to insert HTML code for displaying the data as a dynamic master/detail layout.
    - Select **Insert stacked containers** to insert HTML code for displaying the data in repeating containers stacked one over the other.
    - Select **Insert stacked containers with spotlight area** to insert HTML code for displaying the data in repeating containers stacked one over the other, with a portion of the container highlighted.
    - Select **Do not insert HTML** to avoid inserting HTML code to display data and specify your own layout for the data.
13. If necessary, for the selected display option, click **Set Up,** set the options and click **OK**.
14. Click **Done** to create the data set and display it.

Procedure Reference: Insert a Spry HTML Data Set

To insert a Spry HTML data set:
1. Open an HTML file and place the insertion point where you want to insert the HTML data set.
2. Display the **Spry Data Set** wizard.
3. From the **Select Data Type** drop-down list, select **HTML.**
4. In the **Data Set Name** text box, type a name for the data set.
5. If necessary, from the **Detect** drop-down list, select the HTML element that contains the data.
6. Next to the **Specify Data File** text box, click **Browse,** navigate to and select the **HTML** file that contains data, and click **OK**.

7. Select a data container.
   - From the **Data Containers** drop-down list, select the ID to display a preview of the data set in the **Data Preview** section.
   - Or, in the **Data Selection** text box, click the yellow marker next to the data container to select it and display a preview of the data set in the **Data Preview** text box.
8. If necessary, perform advanced selection.
   a. Check the **Advanced data selection** check box to specify CSS data selectors for the data set.
   b. In the **Row Selectors** text box, type the selectors for the rows to be included.
   c. In the **Column Selectors** text box, type the selectors for the columns to be included.
9. Click **Next.**
10. If necessary, select a column.
    - In the **Data Preview** text box, click the heading of a column.
    - Click the **Select next column** button to select the column on the right of the current column.
    - Click the **Select previous column** button to select the column on the left of the current column.
    - From the **Column Name** drop-down list, select a column.
11. If necessary, from the **Type** drop-down list, select the data type for the selected column.
12. If necessary, from the **Sort Column** drop-down list, select a column to sort the data set.
13. If necessary, from the drop-down list to the right of the **Sort Column** drop-down list, select the direction you want to use to sort the data set.
14. If necessary, set the data options.
    - Check the **Use first row as header** check box to use the data in the first row as the header information.
    - Check the **Use columns as rows** check box to interchange the rows and columns.
    - Check the **Filter out duplicate rows** check box to avoid displaying duplicate rows of data.
    - Check the **Disable Data caching** check box to avoid creating a cache of the data and use the current data in the data set.
    - Check the **Autorefresh Data** check box, and in the text box to the right, specify the time in milliseconds to refresh the data at the specified interval.
15. Click **Next.**
16. In the **Choose Insert Options** section, select a display option.
17. If necessary, for the selected display option, click **Set Up,** set the options and click **OK.**
18. Click **Done** to create the data set and display it.

ACTIVITY 4-4
Displaying XML Data Using Spry

Data Files:

products.html, products.xml

Before You Begin:

From the **FILES** panel, open the products.html file.

Scenario:

You want to add a web page to display the company's products. You feel that maintaining the product data separately and displaying it dynamically on the page will enable you to easily update the pages whenever necessary.

What You Do	How You Do It
1. Specify the data source.	a. Choose **Window→Bindings** to display the **BINDINGS** panel. b. Click the **CSS STYLES** tab to minimize the **CSS STYLES** panel group. c. In the **BINDINGS** panel, click the Plus button (**+**), and choose **Spry Data Set** to open the **Spry Data Set** wizard. d. In the **Spry Data Set** dialog box, from the **Select Data Type** drop-down list, select **XML**. e. In the **Data Set Name** text box, double-click and type *dsproducts* f. To the right of the **Specify Data File** text box, click **Browse**. g. Select **products.xml** and click **OK**. h. Observe that the structure of data in the XML file is displayed in the **Row element** list box. i. In the **Row element** list box, select **product**. j. Observe that the data for each product is displayed in the **Data Preview** section and click **Next**.
2. Specify the data options.	a. In the **Other Options** section, from the **Sort Column** drop-down list, select **name**. b. In the drop-down list to the right of the **Sort Column** drop-down list, verify that **Ascending** is selected and click **Next**. c. In the **Choose Insert Options** section, verify that **Do not insert HTML** is selected and click **Done**. d. Observe that the **BINDINGS** panel displays the data elements from the XML file.

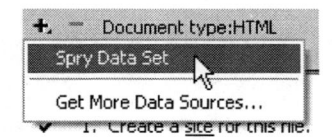

3. Enclose the table in a Spry Region.

    a. In the document window, in the table, click after the text "Name".

    b. Select the table.

    c. Choose **Insert→Spry→Spry Region.**

    d. In the **Insert Spry Region** dialog box, verify that in the **Spry Data Set** drop-down list, **dsproducts** is selected, and click **OK.**

    e. On the status bar, observe that a `<div>` tag is inserted, enclosing the table.

    `<div#text> <div> <table.tbody>`

4. Add data elements from the **BINDINGS** panel.

    a. In the document window, click in the last column of the **Name** row.

    b. In the **BINDINGS** panel, select **name** and click **Insert** to insert the **name** data element into the table.

    c. In the document window, click in the last column of the **Description** row.

    d. In the **BINDINGS** panel, select **desc** and click **Insert** to insert the **desc** data element into the table.

    e. Similarly, insert the **size, cost,** and **rating** data elements in the **Download size, Cost,** and **User rating** rows, respectively.

    f. In the document window, select the image placeholder.

    g. In the **BINDINGS** panel, select **image,** and at the bottom of the panel, in the **Bind to** drop-down list, verify that **img.src** is selected, and click **Bind** to attach the **image** data element to the image placeholder.

5.	Preview the web page using Live view.	a.	On the document toolbar, click **Live View**.
		b.	In the document window, observe that the information for only one product is displayed on the page.
		c.	Click **Live View** to close the preview of the page and return to Design view.
6.	Enclose the table in a Spry Repeat Region.	a.	In the document window, in the table, click after the text "Name".
		b.	Select the table.
		c.	Choose **Insert→Spry→Spry Repeat**.
		d.	In the **Insert Spry Repeat** dialog box, verify that in the **Spry Data Set** drop-down list, **dsproducts** is selected, and click **OK**.
7.	Preview the web page.	a.	Save the products.html file.
		b.	In the **Copy Dependent Files** message box, click **OK**.
		c.	On the document toolbar, click **Live View**.
		d.	In the document window, scroll down.
		e.	Observe that information for all the products is displayed on the page.
		f.	Click **Live View** to close the preview.
		g.	Close the products.html file.

ACTIVITY 4-5
Displaying HTML Data Using Spry

Data Files:

newproducts.html, ourcompany.html

Before You Begin:
From the **FILES** panel, open the ourcompany.html file.

Scenario:
You want to add information about the new products on the Our Company page. Rather than displaying it in the same format as it is displayed on the New Products page, you want to display it in a compact and visually appealing manner. You also want to ensure that any modifications on the New Products page are updated dynamically here.

What You Do	How You Do It
1. Insert an HTML data set.	a. In the document window, scroll down, and click below the subheading text "Latest Products".
	b. In the **INSERT** panel, scroll to the top, and click **Spry Data Set.**
	c. In the **Spry Data Set** dialog box, in the **Select Data Type** drop-down list, verify that **HTML** is selected.
	d. In the **Data Set Name** text box, double-click and type *dsnewproducts*
	e. In the **Detect** drop-down list, verify that **Tables** is selected.
	f. To the right of the **Specify Data File** text box, click **Browse.**
	g. In the **Select file source** dialog box, click **Site Root,** select **newproducts.html,** and click **OK.**
	h. Observe that the content of the HTML file is displayed in the **Data Selection** section.

2. Set the data options.

    a. From the **Data Containers** drop-down list, select **newproducts.**

    b. In the **Data Selection** section, observe that the **newproducts** table is selected, and in the **Data Preview** section, observe that the data from the table is displayed, and click **Next.**

    c. In the **Other Options** section, verify that the **Use first row as header** check box is checked.

    d. Check the **Use columns as rows** check box and click **Next.**

3. Specify the layout details.

    a. In the **Choose Insert Options** section, select **Insert master/detail layout** to display the selected data as a dynamic master/detail layout.

    b. Click **Set Up.**

    c. In the **Spry Data Set - Insert Master/Detail Layout** dialog box, in the **Master Columns** list box, verify that **Product_Name** is displayed.

    d. In the **Detail Columns** list box, in the **Column** column, select **column1,** and above the list box, click the Minus button (**-**) to avoid the images being displayed.

    e. In the **Column** column, verify that **Description** is selected, and from the **Container Type** drop-down list, select **<P>** to use a para tag as the container.

    f. Similarly, set the container type for the **Download_size** and **Cost** columns as **<P>.**

    g. Click **OK.**

    h. In the **Spry Data Set** dialog box, click **Done** to display the Spry HTML data set on the Our Company page.

4. Add labels for the dynamic data display.

    a. In the document window, in the Spry data set, click before the text "{Download size}", type **Download Size:** and press the **Spacebar.**

    b. Click before the text "{Cost}", type **Cost:** and press the **Spacebar.**

5.	Preview the file.	a.	On the **Document** toolbar, click **Live View.**
		b.	Scroll down and click **OGC HR Administrator 1.0** to display the information for the product.
		c.	Click **Live View** to close the preview.
6.	Modify the product information.	a.	In the **FILES** panel, scroll up, and double-click **newproducts.html.**
		b.	In the document window, scroll down, and in the second cell of the **Download size** row, select the text "**8.74 MB**" and type ***9.45 MB***
		c.	Save and close the newproducts.html file.
		d.	Save the ourcompany.html file.
		e.	In the **Copy Dependent Files** message box, click **OK.**
		f.	On the **Document** toolbar, click **Live View.**
		g.	In the document window, scroll down to view the data set.
		h.	Observe that the download size for OGC Contact Manager 1.0 is dynamically updated.
		i.	Click **Live View** to close the preview.
		j.	Close the ourcompany.html file.

Lesson 4 Follow-up

In this lesson, you worked with Spry elements. Using Spry elements, you can present content on a web page effectively and also update web pages with dynamic data.

1. **Which Spry widgets would you use on your web pages? Why?**

2. **Why would you use Spry data sets on your pages?**

5 Creating a Form

Lesson Time: 55 minutes

Lesson Objectives:

In this lesson, you will create and validate forms.

You will:
- Set up a form.
- Add form elements.
- Validate a form.

Introduction

You worked with Spry elements on web pages. You may now need to collect information from your site visitors. In this lesson, you will create forms.

Allowing visitors to your website to provide responses will make your website more interesting. It will also help collect information about site visitors and their views about the site. Creating forms will help you achieve this.

TOPIC A
Set Up a Form

You presented information on your website using various Spry elements. You may now need to let visitors of your site to interact with you by providing information and feedback. In this topic, you will set up a form.

In your business, you may have used paper forms to obtain information from your customers. Though a paper form allows customers to quickly fill in necessary details in a predefined format, it is very difficult to consolidate and infer results from it. By using an electronic form on a web page, you will have a permanent record of the data collected from visitors and be able to generate results in the desired format.

Forms

Definition:

A *form* is an element that gathers data from users and submits it to a server for processing. Each form is identified within a web page by its unique name. It contains form elements, also called controls, and other HTML elements. It supplies the browser with the path to the page or script that will process data and the method to be used for data transmission. Forms differ in the combination of form elements they contain and the scripts that process the data they send.

Example:

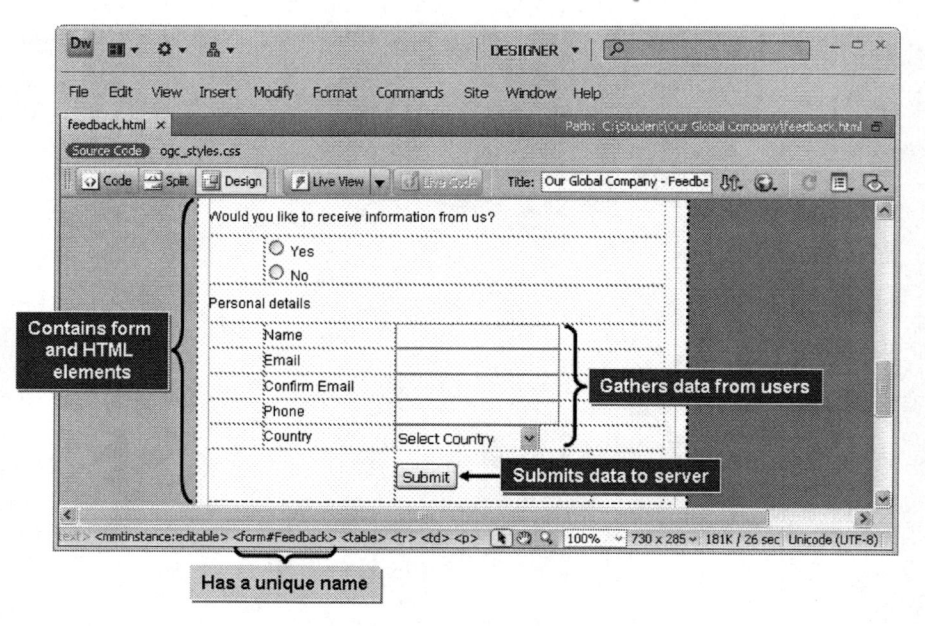

Figure 5-1: A form to collect feedback from site visitors.

Form Properties

Form properties determine the characteristics of a form and specify what happens when the form is submitted.

The table describes the form properties.

Property	Description
Form ID	A unique name that identifies a form on a web page.
Action	The path to a page or script that will process the form.
Method	The way the form's data is submitted to the server. The **GET** method adds the form's data to the URL of the page to which the form's data is sent for processing. The **POST** method embeds the data into the HTTP request sent to the server.
Target	The window in which the data sent back after processing has to be displayed.
Enctype	The MIME encoding type of the submitted data.
Class	The CSS style to be applied to the form.

The GET and POST Methods

The **GET** and **POST** methods specify the method in which information entered in an HTML form is submitted. When a **GET** method is used, the form data is encoded by the browser into a URL and sent to the web server. The **POST** method, when used, transmits the data as part of a message body prepared using a client side script. The **GET** method is usually used when the form data is short and the response required is just an input. The **POST** method is used for long forms, and when the action on submission of the form involves storing or processing the data.

Form Processing Methods

Form processing methods are the different ways in which information in a form is processed. When a form is submitted, the form's data may be sent to an email address, a server-side application page, or a CGI script. When the form's data is sent to an email address, the recipient receives the data in an email message and processes it. When a server-side application page, such as a ColdFusion or JSP page, processes data, it generally searches and updates a database table and returns the results to the browser in HTML. A CGI script processes data in the same way as a server-side application page does and then redirects the request to another HTML page to be returned to the browser.

How to Set Up a Form

Procedure Reference: Create a Form

To create a form:

1. Position the insertion point at a location.
2. Insert the form.
   - Choose **Insert→Form→Form.**
   - Or, in the **INSERT** panel, from the drop-down list, select **Forms,** and click **Form.**
3. If necessary, choose **View→Visual Aids→Invisible Elements** to view a dotted outline for the form.
4. If necessary, insert a table into the form to lay out the form elements.
5. If necessary, modify the table according to the design of the form.

Procedure Reference: Configure the Properties of a Form

To configure the properties of a form:

1. Select the form.
   - Click the dotted line around the form.
   - Or, on the status bar, in the tag selector, select the **<form>** tag.
2. If necessary, in the **Property Inspector,** in the **Form ID** text box, replace the default name with a new name for the form.
3. Specify the page or script for processing the form.
   - In the **Action** text box, type the path to the required page or script.
   - Or, to the right of the **Action** text box, click the folder icon and navigate to the required page or script.
4. From the **Method** drop-down list, select a form processing method.
5. If necessary, from the **Enctype** drop-down list, select the MIME encoding type.

ACTIVITY 5-1
Setting Up a Form

Data Files:

feedback.html

Before You Begin:

1. From the **FILES** panel, open the feedback.html file.
2. Collapse the **CSS STYLES** panel.
3. Collapse the **BINDINGS** panel.

Scenario:

The customer relationship team has suggested that site visitors be allowed to provide feedback about the company's site. The team also wants to collect information from prospective clients about their interests in the company's products.

What You Do	How You Do It
1. Apply a template to the feedback page.	a. In the document window, observe that the text content for the form is displayed in a table.
	b. Choose **Modify→Templates→Apply Template to Page**.
	c. In the **Select Template** dialog box, in the **Templates** list box, select **OGCNewLayout** and click **Select**.
	d. In the **Inconsistent Region Names** dialog box, in the list box, select **Document body**.
	e. From the **Move content to new region** drop-down list, select **MainText**.
	f. In the list box, select **Document head**.
	g. From the **Move content to new region** drop-down list, select **head** and click **OK**.
	h. Observe that the layout used on the other pages of the site is applied to the feedback page.

Lesson 5: Creating a Form 119

2.	Insert a form on the page.	a.	Click after the heading text "Feedback" and press **Enter.**
		b.	In the **INSERT** panel, from the drop-down list, select **Forms** and click **Form.**
		c.	Observe that a form HTML element has been added below the heading.
3.	Set the form properties.	a.	In the **Property Inspector,** in the **Form ID** text box, double-click and type **Feedback** to assign an ID for the form.
		b.	In the **Action** text box, click and type ***mailto:info@ourglobalcompany.com?subject=Feedback***
		c.	In the **Method** drop-down list, verify that **POST** is selected.
4.	Move the content into the form element.	a.	In the table, in the first row, click at the beginning of the text "How long did you spend on the site?"
		b.	On the status bar, in the tag selector, select **<table>** to select the entire table.
		c.	Choose **Edit→Cut.**
		d.	Click in the Feedback form container.
		e.	Choose **Edit→Paste** to move the table into the form container.
		f.	Save the file.

TOPIC B
Add Form Elements

You created a form and set its properties. You may now need to add elements to the form to enable user interaction through collection of information. In this topic, you will add form elements.

While using a form to collect input from site visitors, it is often necessary to provide the right type of input fields to collect the required information. Adding suitable form elements to a form will allow users to enter information in the relevant fields.

Form Elements

A *form element* allows users to interact directly with a form and record their inputs. Identified within a form by a unique name, the form element stores the value the user has entered. When the user submits a form, the name and value pairs of the form elements are sent to the server for processing.

> Form elements can be formatted using CSS styles.

Types of Form Elements

Dreamweaver provides different types of form elements. These types are described in the table.

Type	Description
Text Field	Accepts alphanumeric input.
Hidden Field	Invisible to the user, it stores the information the user has entered in other fields, such as names and email addresses, that can be used by the script that processes the form.
Textarea	Accepts multiple lines of alphanumeric input.
Checkbox	Represents one option that can be selected or deselected.
Checkbox Group	Houses a group of options, each of which can be selected or deselected. Multiple options within a group can be selected.
Radio Button	Represents one option within a group of exclusive options.
Radio Group	Houses a group of radio buttons representing exclusive options. All options in the group share the same name but have different values associated with them. Selecting one option in the group deselects all the others.

Type	Description
List/Menu	Provides either a drop-down list that allows the user to select a single item, or a list box that allows the user to select a single item or multiple items.
Jump Menu	Creates a menu that allows the user to choose an option for navigating to another page.
Image Field	Inserts an image that can serve as a graphical button.
File Field	Allows the user to browse for a file and select it.
Button	Performs a specific task when clicked. Used to submit a form, reset its contents, or execute a script.
Label	Displays descriptive text.
Fieldset	Groups similar form elements.

How to Add Form Elements

Procedure Reference: Add Form Elements

To add form elements:

> This procedure can be followed only for inserting form elements of the type Text Field, Textarea, Check box, Radio Button, List/Menu, File Field, and Button.

1. In the form, position the insertion point at the location where you want to add the form element.
2. Insert the form element.
   - Choose **Insert→Form** and then select a form element.
   - Or, in the **INSERT** panel, from the drop-down list, select **Forms** and then click a form element.
3. In the **Input Tag Accessibility Attributes** dialog box, in the **ID** text box, type an ID for the element.
4. In the **Label** text box, type a label to identify the element.
5. In the **Style** section, select an option for specifying how the label would be associated with the element.
6. If necessary, in the **Position** section, select an option for specifying the position of the label with respect to the element.
7. If necessary, in the **Access key** text box, specify the keyboard equivalent required to access the element.
8. If necessary, in the **Tab Index** text box, specify the tab order of the element.
9. Click **OK** to add the element to the form.

10. If necessary, set the properties of the form element.
    a. In the form, select the form element.
    b. In the **Property Inspector,** set the values for the properties.

The Input Tag Accessibility Attributes Dialog Box

The **Input Tag Accessibility Attributes** dialog box is used to make form elements accessible. The dialog box appears when a new form element is added to a form. Providing information in the dialog box helps to improve the accessibility for site visitors using screen readers.

Procedure Reference: Add a Checkbox Group

To add a checkbox group:

1. Insert a checkbox group form element at a location in the form.
2. If necessary, in the **Checkbox Group** dialog box, in the Name text box, replace the default name with a name for the radio group.
3. In the **Checkboxes** section, in the **Label** column, in the first row, click the default label and type a label name.
4. In the **Value** column, in the first row, click the default value and type a value.
5. In the second row, replace the existing label and value with the desired label and value.
6. If necessary, add check boxes to the group.
    a. In the **Checkboxes** section, click the Plus button (+) to add a check box to the group.
    b. In the **Label** column, click the default label and type a label.
    c. In the **Value** column, click the default value and type a value.
7. If necessary, select a check box and change its order within the group.
    - Click the up arrow button to move the check box one step up in the group.
    - Click the down arrow button to move the check box one step down in the group.
8. If necessary, select the required check box and click the Minus button (-) to remove it from the group.
9. In the **Lay out using** section, select an option to specify the method for aligning the check boxes within the group.
10. Click **OK** to add the checkbox group to the form.

Procedure Reference: Add a Radio Group

To add a radio group:

1. Insert a radio group form element at a location in the form.
2. If necessary, in the **Radio Group** dialog box, in the Name text box, replace the default name with the desired name for the radio group.
3. In the **Radio Buttons** section, in the **Label** column, in the first row, click the default label and type the new label name.
4. In the **Value** column, in the first row, click the default value and type a value.
5. In the second row, replace the existing label and value with the desired label and value.

6. If necessary, add additional radio buttons to the group.
   a. In the **Radio buttons** section, click the Plus button (+) to add a radio button to the group.
   b. In the **Label** column, click the default label and type a label.
   c. In the **Value** column, click the default value and type a value.
7. If necessary, select a radio button and change its order within the group.
   - Click the up arrow button to move the radio button one step up in the group.
   - Click the down arrow button to move the radio button one step down in the group.
8. If necessary, select the required radio button and click the Minus button (-) to remove it from the group.
9. In the **Lay out using** section, select an option to specify the method for aligning the radio buttons within the group.
10. Click **OK** to add the radio group to the form.

Procedure Reference: Set the Properties of a Text Field

To set the properties of a text field:
1. In the form, select the text field for which the properties are to be set.
2. If necessary, in the **Property Inspector,** in the **TextField** text box, replace the existing name of the text field with a new name.
3. In the **Char width** text box, specify the number of characters to be displayed in the text field.
4. In the **Type** section, select an option for specifying the type of the text box.
5. In the **Max chars** text box, specify the maximum number of characters that can be entered in the text field.
6. If necessary, in the **Init val** text box, specify the initial value of the text field.
7. If necessary, from the **Class** drop-down list, select a CSS style to be applied to the text field.

Types of Text Fields

There are three types of text fields:
- **Single line**—The default text field that accepts a single line of text.
- **Multi line**—Equivalent to a text area. The **Num lines** property specifies the number of lines the text field can hold, and the **Wrap** property specifies the wrapping of text.
- **Password**—A text field that masks input with asterisks.

Procedure Reference: Set the Properties of a Check Box or Radio Button

To set the properties of a check box or radio button:
1. In the form, select a check box or radio button to set its properties.
2. If necessary, in the **Property Inspector,** modify the name.
3. In the **Checked value** text box, specify the value that has to be set when the element is selected.
4. In the **Initial state** section, select an option for specifying whether the element is checked or unchecked initially.
5. If necessary, from the **Class** drop-down list, select a CSS style to be applied to the element.

Procedure Reference: Set the Properties of a List

To set the properties of a list:

1. In the form, select a list.
2. If necessary, in the **Property Inspector,** in the **List/Menu** text box, replace the existing name of the list with a new name.
3. In the **Type** section, specify the type of list.
   - Select **Menu** to display a drop-down list.
   - Select **List** to display a list box.
4. Click **List Values.**
5. In the **List Values** dialog box, in the **Item Label** column, type the item name.
6. In the **Value** column, type the value of the item.
7. If necessary, click the Plus button (+) to add another list item and specify its name and value.
8. If necessary, select the required item and click the Minus button (-) to remove it.
9. If necessary, select the required item and modify its order within the list.
10. Click **OK.**

> A list box has two additional properties: Height and Selections. The Height property lets you specify the number of items visible in the list box, and the Selections property lets you specify whether the list box allows a single item or multiple items to be selected.

11. In the **Initially selected** list box, select the item that needs to be selected when the form loads.
12. If necessary, from the **Class** drop-down list, select a CSS style to be applied to the list.

Procedure Reference: Set the Properties of a Button

To set the properties of a button:

1. In the form, select a button.
2. If necessary, in the **Property Inspector,** in the **Button name** text box, replace the existing name with a new name for the button.
3. If necessary, in the **Value** text box, replace the existing text with the text that needs to appear on the button.
4. In the **Action** section, select an option for specifying what should happen when the button is clicked.
5. If necessary, from the **Class** drop-down list, select a CSS style to be applied to the element.

Button Actions

The **Action** property of a button determines what happens when a button is clicked. Dreamweaver provides three options for specifying this property:

- **Submit form**—When the button is clicked, the data in the form is submitted for processing.
- **Reset form**—When the button is clicked, the contents in the form elements are cleared.
- **None**—When the button is clicked, the behavior associated with the button is executed.

ACTIVITY 5-2
Adding Form Elements

Data Files:

feedback.html

Before You Begin:

The feedback.html file is open.

Scenario:

In the form you created, you want visitors to the site to be able to input different types of information to provide feedback about the site. You want to ensure that appropriate fields are available for the user depending on the required information.

What You Do	How You Do It
1. Add a radio group to the form.	a. In the document window, in the second row of the table, click in the second column.
	b. In the **INSERT** panel, click **Radio Group.**
	c. In the **Radio Group** dialog box, in the **Name** text box, type *Time*
	d. In the **Radio buttons** section, in the list box, on the first line, in the **Label** column, click **Radio** and type *Less than 10 minutes* to add a label for the first radio button.
	e. In the **Value** column, click **radio** and type *10min*
	f. Replace the default label and value for the second radio button with the label *10 to 20 minutes* and value *20min*
	g. In the **Radio buttons** section, click the Plus button (+) to add another radio button to the group.
	h. Replace the default label and value for the third radio button with the label *20 to 30 minutes* and value *30min*
	i. In the **Lay out using** section, verify that **Line breaks (tags)** is selected and click **OK** to insert the radio group.

Lesson 5: Creating a Form 127

2. Insert a checkbox group into the form.

   a. In the document window, in the fourth row of the table, click in the second column.

   b. In the **INSERT** panel, click **Checkbox Group.**

   c. In the **Checkbox Group** dialog box, in the **Name** text box, type *Pages*

   d. In the **Checkboxes** section, in the list box, on the first line, in the **Label** column, click **Checkbox** and type *Home*

   e. In the **Value** column, click **checkbox** and type *home*

   f. Replace the default label and value settings for the second check box with the label *Our Company* and value *company*

   g. In the **Checkboxes** section, click the Plus button (+) to add another check box to the group.

   h. Replace the default label and value for the third check box with the label *Clients & Partners* and value *clients*

   i. Similarly, add three check boxes with the labels *News & Events, Careers,* and *Products* with values *news, careers,* and *products.*

   j. In the **Lay out using** section, verify that **Line breaks (
 tags)** is selected and click **OK** to insert the checkbox group.

3. Insert a text area.

   a. In the document window, scroll down, and in the row below the text "Feedback Message", click in the second column.

   b. In the **INSERT** panel, click **Textarea.**

   c. In the **Input Tag Accessibility Attributes** dialog box, in the **ID** text box, type *Message* and click **OK.**

4. Insert a radio group.

   a. In the document window, in the row below the text "Would you like to receive information from us?", click in the second column.

   b. In the **INSERT** panel, click **Radio Group.**

   c. In the **Radio Group** dialog box, in the **Name** text box, type *Information*

   d. In the **Radio buttons** section, in the list box, on the first line, in the **Label** column, click **Radio** and type *Yes* to add a label for the first radio button.

   e. In the **Value** column, click **radio** and type *yes*

   f. Replace the default label and value for the second radio button with the label *No* and value *no*

   g. In the **Lay out using** section, verify that **Line breaks (
 tags)** is selected and click **OK.**

5. Add text fields to the form.

   a. In the document window, scroll down and click in the cell to the right of the cell with the text "Name".

   b. In the **INSERT** panel, click **Text Field.**

   c. In the **Input Tag Accessibility Attributes** dialog box, in the **ID** text box, type *Name* and click **OK.**

   d. In the document window, click in the cell to the right of the cell with the text "Phone".

   e. In the **INSERT** panel, click **Text Field,** and in the **Input Tag Accessibility Attributes** dialog box, in the **ID** text box, type *Phone* and then click **OK.**

6. Add a drop-down list to the form.
   a. In the document window, click in the cell to the right of the cell with the text "Country".

   b. In the **INSERT** panel, click **List/Menu.**

   c. In the **Input Tag Accessibility Attributes** dialog box, in the **ID** text box, type *Country* and click **OK.**

   d. In the document window, click the inserted drop-down list and, in the **Tag Selector**, select **select#Country** to display its properties in the **Property Inspector.**

   e. In the **Property Inspector**, click **List Values.**

   f. In the **List Values** dialog box, in the list box, in the **Item Label** column, type *United States*

   g. In the **Value** column, click and type *us*

   h. Click the Plus button (+), and in the list box, in the **Item Label** column, type *Canada*

   i. In the **Value** column, click and type *ca*

   j. Similarly, add the list values *Mexico, Japan, France, Germany* and *United Kingdom* with the values **me, ja, fr, ge,** and **uk,** respectively.

   k. In the **List Values** dialog box, click **OK.**

7. Add a button to submit the form.
   a. In the document window, in the last row of the table, click in the second cell.

   b. In the **INSERT** panel, click **Button.**

   c. In the **Input Tag Accessibility Attributes** dialog box, in the **ID** text box, type *Submit* and click **OK.**

   d. Save the feedback.html file.

TOPIC C
Validate a Form

You inserted form elements to collect different types of inputs. You may now need a mechanism that helps check whether the inputs are valid. In this topic, you will validate forms.

Having designed form elements to collect specific information, you need to ensure that the user provides valid values in them. You can accomplish this by validating forms.

Form Validation

Form validation refers to the task of checking whether the user has entered the required data in the form and whether the data entered is valid. It can be performed either on the client or on the server. On the client, form validation is performed by scripts using JavaScript or by Spry form validation widgets. On the server, form validation is performed by script written to process the form.

Spry Form Validation Widgets

Spry form validation widgets are Spry form elements that allow user inputs and also validate the form elements. You can specify the validation options and the event on which the validation must occur. Dreamweaver provides seven Spry form validation widgets.

These widgets are described in the table.

Widget	Description
Spry Validation Text Field	A text field that validates user input for the specific type, format, and value.
Spry Validation Textarea	A text area that validates user input for the number of characters. It has a character count and allows input only above the minimum limit and within the maximum limit.
Spry Validation Checkbox	A check box, or a group of check boxes, that validates whether the user has made the required number of selections.
Spry Validation Select	A drop-down list that checks whether or not the user's selection is valid.
Spry Validation Password	A password text field that validates the user's input for specified password criteria. Criteria can be specified for maximum and minimum number of letters, numbers, special characters, and uppercase letters allowed.
Spry Validation Confirm	A text field that validates the user's input to match another field in the form such as an email field or a password field.
Spry Validation Radio Group	A group of radio buttons that checks whether the user has selected at least one option.

The Validate Form Behavior

The **Validate Form** behavior helps ensure that the user has entered the correct type of data by checking the values specified in the text fields and text areas in a form. It is usually attached to the **onSubmit** event to validate user input when the form is submitted.

Types of Data

The **Validate Form** behavior can validate the following types of data:

- **Number**—Validates the input for digits. Rejects the form submission if any other characters are typed.
- **Number from**—Validates the input for a number in a specific range. Rejects the form submission if the input is outside the range.
- **Email address**—Checks whether the input has an @ symbol. Rejects the form submission if the @ symbol is not found.
- **Anything**—Accepts any type of data. Rejects form submission if no data is entered.

How to Validate a Form

Procedure Reference: Add a Spry Form Validation Widget

To add a Spry form validation widget:

> This procedure can be followed only for inserting Spry form validation widgets of the type Spry Validation Text Field, Spry Validation Textarea, Spry Validation Checkbox, Spry Validation Select, Spry Validation Password, and Spry Validation Confirm.

1. In the form, position the insertion point at the location where you want to add the Spry form validation widget.
2. Insert the Spry form validation widget.
    - Choose **Insert→Spry** and then select a Spry form validation widget.
    - Or, in the **INSERT** panel, from the drop-down list, select **Forms** and then click a Spry form validation widget.
3. In the **Input Tag Accessibility Attributes** dialog box, in the **ID** text box, type an ID for the widget.
4. In the **Label** text box, type a label to identify the widget.
5. In the **Style** section, select an option for specifying how the label is associated with the widget.
6. If necessary, in the **Position** section, select an option for specifying the position of the label with respect to the widget.
7. If necessary, in the **Access key** text box, specify the key required to access the widget.
8. If necessary, in the **Tab Index** text box, specify the tab order of the widget.
9. Click **OK** to add the widget to the form.
10. If necessary, set the properties of the widget.
    a. In the form, select the widget.
    b. In the **Property Inspector,** set the properties.

Procedure Reference: Add a Spry Validation Radio Group Widget

To add a **Spry Validation Radio Group** widget:

1. In the form, position the insertion point at the location where you want to add the **Spry Validation Radio Group** widget.
2. Insert the **Spry Validation Radio Group** widget.
   - Choose **Insert**→**Spry**→**Spry Validation Radio Group**.
   - Or, in the **INSERT** panel, from the drop-down list, select **Forms** and then click **Spry Validation Radio Group**.
3. If necessary, in the **Radio Group** dialog box, in the **Name** text box, replace the default name with a name for the radio group.
4. In the **Radio Buttons** section, in the **Label** column, in the first row, click the default label and type a label.
5. In the **Value** column, in the first row, click the default value and type a value.
6. In the second row, replace the existing label and value with the desired label and value.
7. If necessary, add additional radio buttons to the group.
   a. In the **Radio buttons** section, click the Plus button (+) to add a radio button to the group.
   b. Specify a label name and value for each radio button.
8. If necessary, select a radio button and change its order within the group.
   - Click the up arrow button to move the radio button one step up in the group.
   - Click the down arrow button to move the radio button one step down in the group.
9. If necessary, select the required radio button and click the Minus button (-) to remove it from the group.
10. In the **Lay out using** section, select an option to specify the method for aligning the radio buttons within the group.
11. Click **OK** to add the radio group to the form.

Procedure Reference: Set the Properties of a Spry Validation Widget

To set the properties of a Spry validation widget:

1. In the form, select a Spry validation widget.
2. If necessary, in the **Property Inspector,** in the **Spry <widget name>** text box, replace the existing name with a new name.
3. Specify the validation criteria for the Spry validation widget.
   - Specify the criteria for the Spry Validation Text Field widget.
     a. From the **Type** drop-down list, select an option for specifying the type of information the text field will hold.
     b. If necessary, from the **Format** drop-down list, select an option for specifying the data format for the specified type.
     c. If necessary, in the **Pattern** text box, type a custom pattern to specify the input pattern.
     d. If necessary, in the **Hint** text box, type the text that will be displayed as a hint to the user.
     e. In the **Min chars** and **Max chars** text boxes, specify the minimum and maximum number of characters required in the text field.

f. Check the **Enforce pattern** check box to prevent users from typing invalid characters in the text field.
- Specify the criteria for the Spry Validation Password widget.
    a. In the **Min chars** and **Max chars** text boxes, specify the minimum and maximum number of characters required in the password.
    b. If necessary, specify more password criteria.
        - In the **Min letters** and **Max letters** text boxes, specify the minimum number of letters required and the maximum number of letters that the password can contain.
        - In the **Min numbers** and **Max numbers** text boxes, specify the minimum number of numbers required and the maximum number of numbers that the password can contain.
        - In the **Min uppercase** and **Max uppercase** text boxes, specify the minimum number of uppercase letters required and the maximum number of uppercase letters that the password can contain.
        - In the **Min special chars** and **Max special chars** text boxes, specify the minimum number of special characters required and the maximum number of special characters that the password can contain.
- For the Spry Validation Confirm widget, from the **Validate against** drop-down list, select the form element the Spry Validation Confirm widget is to be matched against.
- Specify the criteria for the Spry Validation Radio Group widget.
    a. In the **Empty Value** text box, specify a value that renders radio buttons associated with that value as empty selections.
    b. In the **Invalid Value** text box, specify a value that renders radio buttons associated with that value as invalid selections.
4. From the **Preview states** drop-down list, select the desired state.
5. In the **Validate on** section, check a check box to specify the event at which the validation should occur.
6. If necessary, check the **Required** check box if user input is required in the text field.

Procedure Reference: Add a Behavior to Validate a Form

To add a behavior to validate a form:
1. Select the form.
2. Open the **TAG INSPECTOR** panel.
3. Click **Behavior** to display the behavior options.
4. Click the **Add behavior** button and choose **Validate Form.**
5. In the **Validate Form** dialog box, in the **Fields** list box, select a form element.
6. If necessary, in the **Value** section, check the **Required** check box to specify that a value is required in this field.
7. In the **Accept** section, select an option to specify the type of value the element will accept.
8. If necessary, specify validation settings for the other elements in the **Fields** list box.
9. Click **OK.**
10. Save the changes to the web page.

11. In the **Copy Dependent Files** message box, click **OK**.

Procedure Reference: Test a Form

To test a form:

1. In Internet Explorer, preview the web page that contains the form.
2. Fill the fields in the form.
3. Click the **Submit** button to submit the form for processing.
4. If necessary, in the **Microsoft Internet Explorer** message box, click **OK**.
5. If necessary, resubmit the form for processing.
    a. Correct invalid entries or type information in the required fields.
    b. Click the **Submit** button to submit the form again.
6. In the **Microsoft Internet Explorer** message box, click **OK**.

ACTIVITY 5-3
Validating Forms

Data Files:

feedback.html

Before You Begin:

The feedback.html file is open.

Scenario:

In the form you have been developing on the feedback.html web page, you need to collect data such as the feedback type, email, and email confirmation. You need to ensure that users enter valid data and provide information in the email, email confirmation, and phone fields.

What You Do	How You Do It
1. Add a Spry validation radio group to the form.	a. In the document window, scroll up, and in the row below the text "Feedback type", click in the second column.
	b. In the **INSERT** panel, click **Spry Validation Radio Group.**
	c. In the **Spry Validation Radio Group** dialog box, in the **Name** text box, type *FeedbackType*
	d. In the **Radio buttons** section, in the list box, on the first line, click **Radio** and type *General Feedback* to add a label for the first radio button.
	e. In the **Value** column, click the word **radio** and type *feedback*
	f. Replace the default label and value for the second radio button with the label *Request for Information* and value *info*
	g. In the **Radio buttons** section, click the Plus button (**+**) to add another radio button to the group.
	h. Replace the default label and value for the third radio button with the label *Complaint* and value *complaint*
	i. In the **Lay out using** section, verify that **Line breaks (tags)** is selected and click **OK** to insert the radio group.
	j. In the **Property Inspector,** in the **Spry Radio Group** text box, double-click and type *FeedbackType* and then press **Enter.**

2.	Add a field to collect email addresses of site visitors.	a. In the document window, scroll down and click in the cell to the right of the cell with the text "Email".
		b. In the **INSERT** panel, click **Spry Validation Text Field.**
		c. In the **Input Tag Accessibility Attributes** dialog box, in the **ID** text box, type *Email* and click **OK.**
		d. In the **Property Inspector,** in the **Spry Text Field** text box, double-click and type *EmailAddress* and then press **Enter.**
		e. From the **Type** drop-down list, select **Email Address.**
3.	Add a field for email confirmation.	a. In the document window, click in the cell to the right of the cell with the text "Confirm Email".
		b. In the **INSERT** panel, click **Spry Validation Confirm.**
		c. In the **Input Tag Accessibility Attributes** dialog box, in the **ID** text box, type **ConfirmEmail** and click **OK.**
		d. In the **Property Inspector,** in the **Spry Confirm** text box, double-click and type *EmailConfirm* and then press **Enter.**
		e. In the **Validate against** drop-down list, verify that **"Email" in form "Feedback"** is selected.

4. Add a behavior to validate the form.

    a. In the document window, in the tag selector, select **<form#Feedback>**.

    b. Choose **Window→Behaviors**.

    c. In the **TAG INSPECTOR** panel, click the **Add behavior** button and choose **Validate Form**.

    d. In the **Validate Form** dialog box, in the **Fields** list box, select **input "Email"** and, in the **Value** section, check the **Required** check box.

    e. In the **Accept** section, select **Email address**.

    f. In the **Fields** list box, select **input "ConfirmEmail"**, in the **Value** section, check the **Required** check box, and in the **Accept** section, select **Email address**.

    g. Similarly, set the value of the Phone field as **Required**.

    h. In the **Accept** section, select **Number** and click **OK**.

    i. Save the changes made to the web page.

    j. In the **Copy Dependent Files** message box, click **OK**.

ACTIVITY 5-4
Testing Forms

Data Files:

feedback.html

Before You Begin:

The feedback.html file is open.

Scenario:

You developed the form that will be used to receive feedback from site visitors. Before making this web page available to the visitors of your website, you need to ensure that the form works as intended.

What You Do	How You Do It
1. Fill in the feedback form.	a. Preview the web page in Internet Explorer.
	b. In the Internet Explorer window, scroll down, and in the **Name** text box, click and type **Frank Parker**
	c. In the **Email** text box, click and type *frank_parker@ourglobalcompany.example*
	d. In the **Phone** text box, click and type *2125551100*
	e. Click **Submit** to submit the form for processing.
	f. In the **Microsoft Internet Explorer** message box, observe the message stating that an input is required in the **Confirm Email** text box.
	g. Click **OK** to close the message box.

2. Submit the form with data in all the required fields.

    a. In the **Confirm Email** text box, click and type *frank_parker@ourglobalcompany.example*

    b. Click **Submit** to submit the form for processing.

    c. In the **Microsoft Internet Explorer** message box, click **OK.**

    d. Observe that the form is submitted successfully and no warning messages are displayed.

    e. In the **Outlook Express** message box, click **Do Not Send.**

    f. Close the Internet Explorer window and then close the feedback.html web page.

Lesson 5 Follow-up

In this lesson, you created forms. Creating forms enables users to interact directly with websites, thereby making the websites more engaging and useful.

1. **Which form elements might you use most when designing a form? Why?**

2. **What form validation techniques will you use to check user input in the forms you create?**

6 Integrating External Files with Dreamweaver

Lesson Time: 35 minutes

Lesson Objectives:

In this lesson, you will integrate external files with Dreamweaver.

You will:

- Integrate Photoshop images in Dreamweaver.
- Insert media objects.
- Integrate XML-based data.

Introduction

You created forms on a website. There may be times when you need to insert elements not native to Dreamweaver. In this lesson, you will integrate external files with your web pages.

It may be necessary to add content created in other file formats to your web pages. Adding content directly to your pages will save you the effort and time required to transform it to a format supported by web browsers. It will also be easier to edit content in its native application and automatically update it on web pages. Dreamweaver helps you achieve this by supporting integration with other applications.

TOPIC A
Integrate Photoshop Images in Dreamweaver

You used forms to collect information from site visitors. You may now want to insert images that were created in other image editing applications. In this topic, you will integrate Photoshop images in Dreamweaver.

While developing web pages, you may not have the final image that you will be using on a page. The image may require repeated editing before it is finalized. Saving the image in a web-ready format and manually updating it on the page every time it is modified will be a monotonous task. Using the image in its native format and updating changes to the image within Dreamweaver will help save time. Dreamweaver helps you achieve this by integrating Photoshop images.

Adobe® Photoshop®

Adobe® Photoshop® is an image-editing application developed by Adobe. It is used for creating and editing images. Images created with Photoshop are saved with the .psd extension. The application also supports many other file extensions such as .jpeg, .gif, .bmp, and .png.

The Image Preview Dialog Box

The **Image Preview** dialog box provides options to optimize and transform Photoshop images to web-ready images that can be inserted in a Dreamweaver document. It allows you to specify the image format as JPEG, GIF, or PNG, the image quality, and other optimization settings. It also allows you to resize the image, and crop and export a specific area of the image. The preview section displays how the image will appear with the defined settings and provides information about the size and download time of the image.

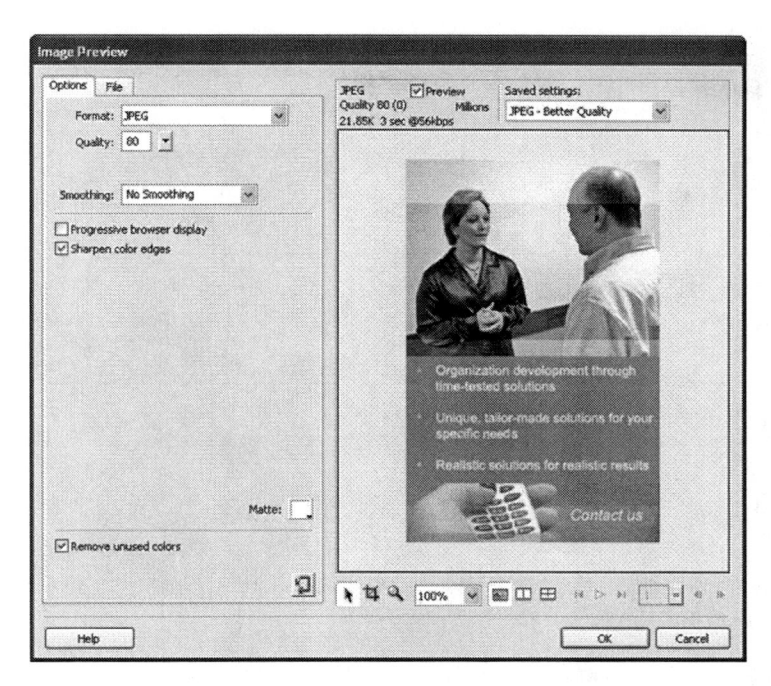

Figure 6-1: The Image Preview dialog box displaying the preview of a Photoshop image.

Smart Objects

Definition:

A *smart object* is a Photoshop image optimized by Dreamweaver and inserted on a web page. It is an instance of the original image and maintains live connection with the original file. It can be identified by a smart object icon with green arrows displayed in its upper-left corner. Whenever the original image is modified, the smart object icon changes to a red arrow. You can then update the image from the original file. However, when a smart object is edited in Dreamweaver, the original image is not altered. You can insert multiple smart objects using a single Photoshop image.

Example:

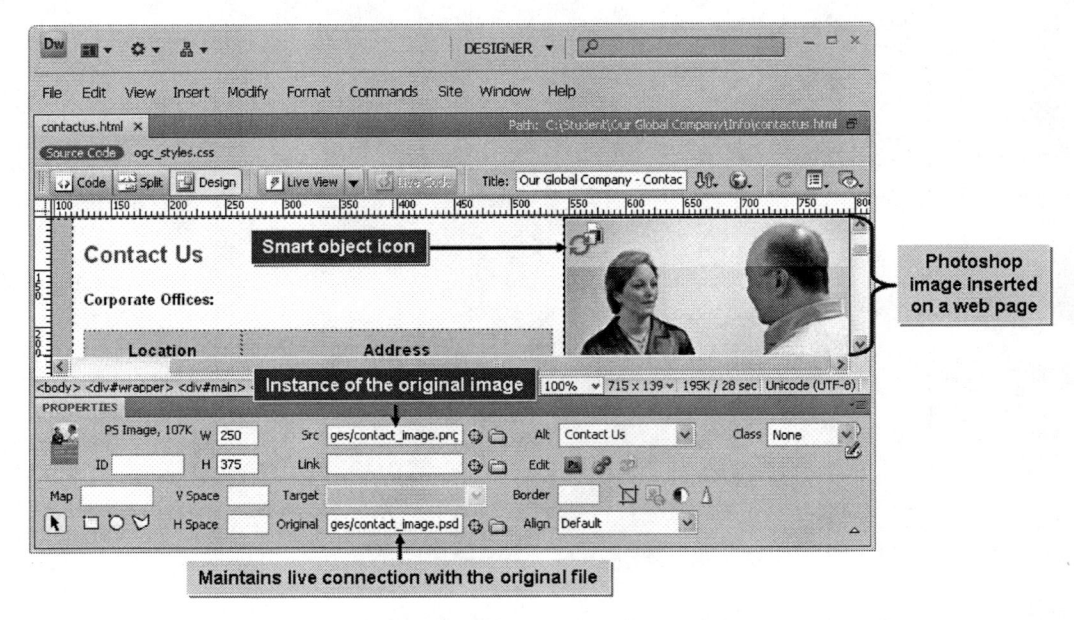

Figure 6-2: A Photoshop smart object inserted on a web page.

How to Integrate Photoshop Images in Dreamweaver

Procedure Reference: Insert a Photoshop Image on a Web Page

To insert a Photoshop image on a web page:

1. In the document window, click in a location to position the insertion point where the image is to be inserted.
2. Display the **Select Image Source** dialog box.
   - Choose **Insert→Image.**
   - Or, in the **INSERT** panel, from the drop-down list, select **Common**, click **Images**, and choose **Image.**
3. Navigate to the folder that contains the Photoshop image.
4. Select the Photoshop image and click **OK** to open the **Image Preview** dialog box.
5. On the **Options** tab, from the **Format** drop-down list, select an image format.
6. If necessary, specify the image optimization settings.
   - In the **Quality** text box, specify the image quality.
   - From the **Smoothing** drop-down list, select an option.
   - Check the **Remove unused colors** check box to remove color information from the file for colors not used in the image.
   - Change the **Matte** color to specify a background color for the image.
   - Click the **Optimize to size wizard** button. In the **Target size** text box, specify the target size for the image and click **OK** to allow Dreamweaver to set the optimization settings.

7. If necessary, resize and crop the image.
   a. Select the **File** tab.
   b. Specify the width and height for the image.
      - Click and drag the % slider to set the scale percentage.
      - In the **W** and **H** text boxes, specify the width and height.
      - Uncheck the **Constrain** check box to allow disproportional scaling of the image.
   c. If necessary, check the **Export area** check box and in the **X, Y, W,** and **H** text boxes, specify the cropping values.
8. If necessary, check the **Preview** check box to display a preview of the image as it would appear on the web page.
9. If necessary, from the **Saved settings** drop-down list, select a preset image optimization setting.
10. Click **OK.**
11. In the **Save Web Image** dialog box, navigate to the folder in which the web image is to be saved.
12. In the **File name** text box, type a name for the image and then click **Save.**
13. In the **Image Tag Accessibility Attributes** dialog box, in the **Alternate text** text box, type alternate text for the image.
14. Click **OK** to insert the Photoshop image on the web page.

Procedure Reference: Update a Photoshop Smart Object on a Web Page

To update a Photoshop smart object on a web page:
1. In the document window, click the Photoshop image with a smart object icon showing a red arrow, indicating that the original file is modified.
2. Update the image.
   - In the **Property Inspector,** click the **Update from Original** button.
   - Or, choose **Modify→Image→Update From Original.**
   - Or, right-click and choose **Update From Original.**
3. Save the web page.

Adobe® Dreamweaver® CS4: Level 2

ACTIVITY 6-1
Inserting a Photoshop Image

Data Files:

contactus.html, contact_image.psd

Before You Begin:
In the **FILES** panel, expand the Info folder, and open the contactus.html file.

Scenario:
Your manager has asked you to add an image to the Contact Us page. The design team has provided you with a Photoshop image. However, you need an image in a web-ready format to insert it on the web page. You also want to ensure that when the original image is modified, the image on the web page can be automatically updated without manually replacing it.

What You Do	How You Do It
1. Select the Photoshop image to be inserted.	a. In the document window, in the container to the right of the main text, click at the top-left corner.
	b. Choose **Insert→Image**.
	c. In the **Select Image Source** dialog box, navigate to the C:\084054Data\Our Global Company\images folder.
	d. Scroll to the right, select **contact_image.psd,** and click **OK**.
2. Insert the image as a smart object.	a. In the **Image Preview** dialog box, on the **Options** tab, from the **Format** drop-down list, select **PNG 24** and click **OK**.
	b. In the **Save Web Image** dialog box, navigate to the C:\084054Data\Our Global Company\images folder.
	c. In the **File name** text box, verify that contact_image.png is displayed and click **Save**.
	d. In the **Image Tag Accessibility Attributes** dialog box, in the **Alternate text** text box, type *Contact Us* and click **OK**.

e. Observe that the smart object icon appears at the top-left corner of the image, indicating that the image is inserted as a Photoshop smart object.

f. Save the contactus.html file.

Adobe® Dreamweaver® CS4: Level 2

ACTIVITY 6-2
Updating a Photoshop Smart Object

Data Files:

contactus.html

Before You Begin:

1. The contactus.html file is open.
2. From the C:\084054Data\Our Global Company\images folder, open the contact_image.psd image in Adobe Photoshop.

Scenario:

Your manager has asked you to remove the link at the bottom of the image on the Contact Us page, because the link is not required on this page. You need to ensure that after modifying the Photoshop image, the image on the web page is also modified.

What You Do	How You Do It
1. Edit the Photoshop image.	a. Double-click the **LAYERS** tab to display the **LAYERS** panel.
	b. In the **LAYERS** panel, for the Contact Us layer, click the eye icon to hide the layer.
	c. Save the file.
	d. Close the Photoshop application.
2. Update the smart object.	a. In the document window, observe that the smart object icon on the image displays a red arrow, indicating that the image has been edited.
	b. In the **Property Inspector,** click the **Update from Original** button.
	c. Observe that the image is updated and the smart object icon displays green arrows.
	d. Save and close the file.

Lesson 6: Integrating External Files with Dreamweaver

TOPIC B
Insert Media Objects

You used Photoshop smart objects on your web pages. You may now want to display content in the form of animations and videos. In this topic, you will insert media objects.

Displaying information through a website using just text and images may often be difficult. You may need to use multimedia elements to convey the message in an effective manner. Using media objects, you can present information effectively.

Media Objects

Media objects are elements such as animation or video files in Flash, Shockwave movies, Java applets, ActiveX controls, or other multimedia formats that are not natively supported by a browser. These elements require an external program to render them in the browser. When media objects are inserted on a web page using Dreamweaver, code required to load these external programs is automatically inserted. Dreamweaver allows you to set the properties and accessibility attributes of these elements.

The Object and Embed Tags

The `object` and `embed` tags are used to render and control media objects on a web page. In addition to the content that needs to be rendered, these tags provide the browser with information about the external program required to render them. Although the tags perform a similar function, Dreamweaver uses them both because, while some browsers support both tags, older versions of other browsers support only the `embed` tag.

How to Insert Media Objects

Procedure Reference: Insert a Flash Movie

To insert a Flash movie:

1. In the document window, click in a location to position the insertion point where the Flash movie is to be inserted.
2. Display the **Select File** dialog box.
   - Choose **Insert→Media→SWF.**
   - Or, in the **INSERT** panel, from the drop-down list, select **Common**, click **Media**, and choose **SWF.**
3. If necessary, navigate to the folder that contains the Flash movie.
4. Select the Flash movie and click **OK**.
5. In the **Object Tag Accessibility Attributes** dialog box, in the **Title** text box, type a title for the Flash movie.
6. If necessary, in the **Access key** text box, specify the key that can be used to access the Flash movie.
7. If necessary, in the **Tab index** text box, type the number of times the **Tab** key has to be pressed to access the Flash movie.
8. Click **OK**.

9. If necessary, preview the Flash movie.
    a. In the **Property Inspector,** click **Play** to play the Flash movie.
    b. Click **Stop** to stop the Flash movie.

Procedure Reference: Insert a Flash Video

To insert a Flash video:
1. In the document window, click in a location to position the insertion point where the Flash video is to be inserted.
2. Display the **Insert FLV** dialog box.
   - Choose **Insert→Media→FLV.**
   - Or, in the **INSERT** panel, from the drop-down list, select **Common**, click **Media,** and choose **FLV.**
3. From the **Video type** drop-down list, select an option.
   - Select **Progressive Download Video** to download the video and simultaneously play it.
   - Select **Streaming Video** to buffer the streamed video content and play it.
4. Specify the location of the Flash video.
   - Specify the URL for the progressive download video.
     - In the **URL** text box, type the URL of the Flash video file.
     - Or, click the **Browse** button, navigate to the folder that contains the Flash video file, select the file, and click **OK.**
   - Specify the URI for the streaming video.
     a. In the **Server URI** text box, specify the server URI.
     b. In the **Stream name** text box, type the file name of the Flash video file.
5. From the **Skin** drop-down list, select an option to define the appearance of the Flash video component.
6. Specify the dimensions of the Flash video.
   - Click **Detect Size** to allow Dreamweaver to determine the exact width and height of the Flash video.
   - If necessary, check the **Constrain** check box to maintain the same aspect ratio of the width and height of the Flash video.
   - If necessary, in the **Width** text box, type the width of the Flash video in pixels.
   - If necessary, in the **Height** text box, type the height of the Flash video in pixels.
7. If necessary, check the **Live video feed** check box to play the live video content directly from the server.
8. If necessary, check the **Auto play** check box to automatically play the Flash video as the web page opens.
9. If necessary, check the **Auto rewind** check box to return the Flash video to the starting position as soon as the video completes playing.
10. If necessary, in the **Buffer time** text box, type the time, in seconds, required for buffering before the video starts playing.
11. Click **OK** to insert the Flash video.

The Server URI

The server URI is used to specify the server name, application name, and instance name from where the video is streamed. The format for defining the server URI is **rtmp:// www.example.com/app_name/instance_name.**

ACTIVITY 6-3
Inserting a Flash Movie

Data Files:

upcomingevents.html

Setup:

From the **FILES** panel, open the upcomingevents.html file.

Scenario:

You designed a fully functional website for your company. However, your manager has suggested that you enhance it to make it more appealing to site visitors. You want to use an animated banner to make the pages visually appealing.

What You Do	How You Do It
1. Replace the header image with a Flash movie.	a. Select the header image and press **Delete**.
	b. Choose **Insert→Media→SWF**.
	c. In the **Select File** dialog box, double-click the **images** folder to open it.
	d. Select the **Banner.swf** file and click **OK**.
	e. In the **Object Tag Accessibility Attributes** dialog box, in the **Title** text box, type *Our Global Company Header* and click **OK**.
2. Preview the movie.	a. In the document window, in the header container, observe that the Flash movie is inserted and appears with a gray background.
	b. In the **Property Inspector**, click **Play** to play the Flash movie.
	c. Click **Stop** to stop playing the SWF file.
	d. Save the web page.
	e. In the **Copy Dependent Files** message box, click **OK**.

ACTIVITY 6-4
Inserting a Flash Video

Data Files:

upcomingevents.html

Before You Begin:

The upcomingevents.html file is open.

Scenario:

The marketing team of your company has identified a sponsor for the upcoming events. You need to include the promotional video provided by the sponsor on the Upcoming Events page.

What You Do	How You Do It
1. Select the Flash video file for insertion.	a. In the document window, scroll down, and in the images container, click below the text "Events sponsor:".
	b. Choose **Insert→Media→FLV** to display the **Insert FLV** dialog box.
	c. In the **Video type** drop-down list, verify that **Progressive Download Video** is selected.
	d. To the right of the **URL** text box, click **Browse.**
	e. In the **Select FLV** dialog box, double-click the **images** folder to open it.
	f. Select the **everythingforcoffee.flv** file and click **OK.**

2.	Set the dimensions of the video display.	a.	In the **Insert FLV** dialog box, click **Detect Size** to obtain the width and the height of the Flash video.
		b.	Verify that the **Constrain** check box is checked.
		c.	In the **Width** text box, double-click, type *240* and press the **Tab** key.
		d.	Observe that the height is changed to 180 in proportion to the width.
		e.	Check the **Auto play** check box to play the video when the page loads, and click **OK**.
3.	Preview the web page using Live View.	a.	Save the file.
		b.	On the **Document** toolbar, click **Live View.**
		c.	Scroll down to the bottom of the page.
		d.	Observe that the Flash video plays on the web page.
		e.	On the **Document** toolbar, click **Live View** again to close the preview.
		f.	Close the upcomingevents.html file.

TOPIC C
Integrate XML-Based Data

You inserted media objects on web pages. You may now want to display data available in XML format. In this topic, you will integrate XML-based data with the web page content.

You may have to present dynamic data on a web page. Data may be stored and maintained separately in XML format. Using Dreamweaver, you can display dynamic data on your pages.

XSL
Definition:

eXtensible Stylesheet Language, or *XSL*, is a style sheet language used to define the presentation of content in a document. The basic function of XSL is to display XML data on a web page. A single style sheet can be applied to multiple pages.

Example:

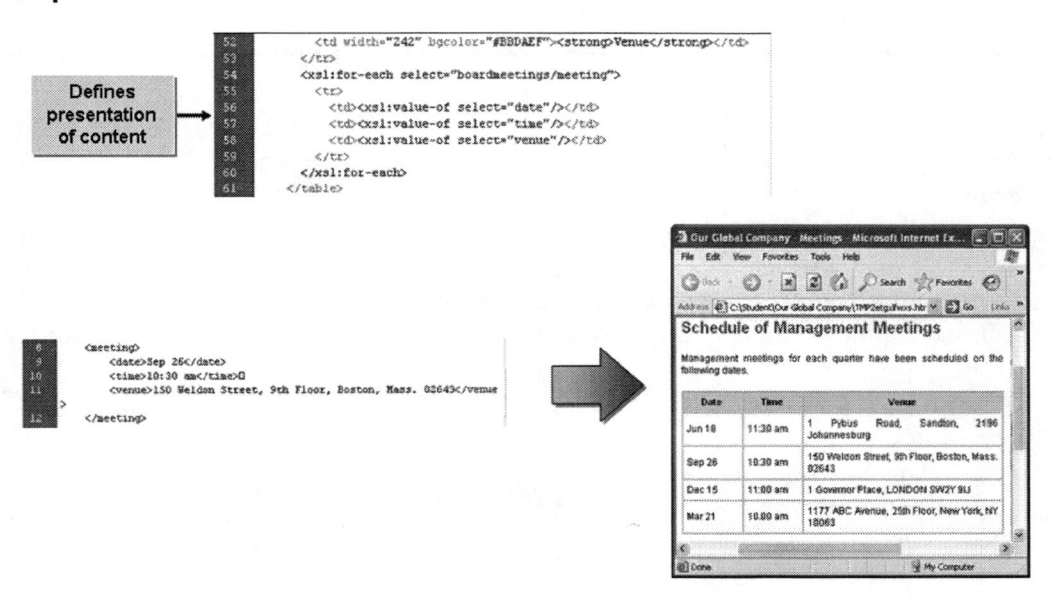

Figure 6-3: XSL used to present XML data on a web page.

The Structure of XSL

XSL is made up of three different languages.

Language	Description
XSLT	eXtensible Stylesheet Language Transformation (XSLT) is the transformation language of XSL. It is used to transform XML documents to other XML formats, or to other languages such as HTML and XHTML.
XSL-FO	eXtensible Stylesheet Language Formatting Objects (XSL-FO) is the formatting language of XSL. It is used to apply formatting styles to the content in XML documents and also to describe how XML data will output to different media.
XPath	XPath is a non-XML expression language. It is used to navigate through an XML document and address different parts of it.

RSS

Definition:

Really Simple Syndication, or *RSS,* is an XML-based data format that allows you to publish dynamic content on a website. It provides a short description of content along with a link to the entire content. When you create a website that will publish content from other sites, it displays XML data on the web page. Using RSS, you can provide up-to-date information for the users.

Example:

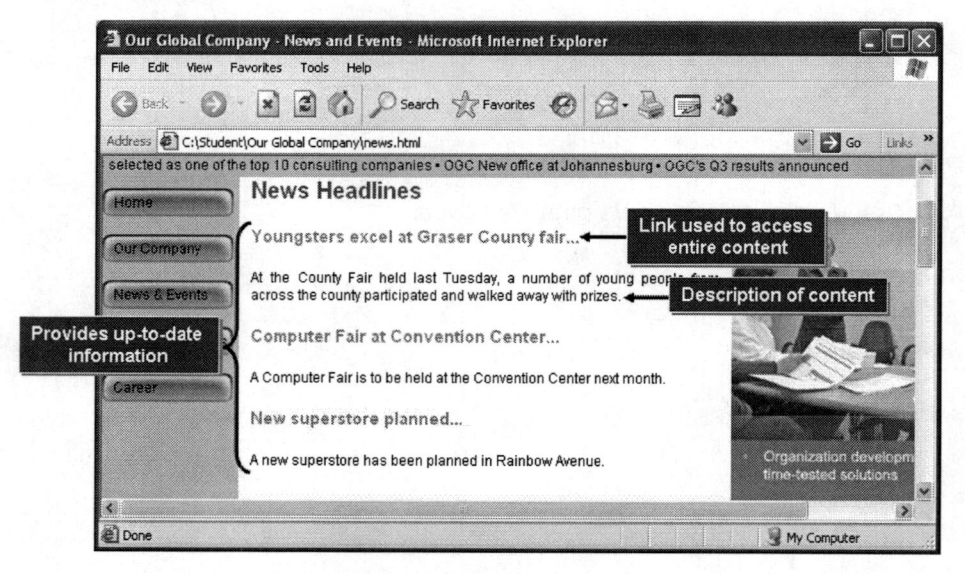

Figure 6-4: RSS content displayed on a web page.

How to Integrate XML-Based Data

Procedure Reference: Convert an HTML File to an XSLT File

To convert an HTML file to an XSLT file:

1. Open an HTML page.
2. Choose **File→Convert→XSLT 1.0** to convert the HTML file into an XSLT file.

> It is necessary to convert an HTML file to an XSLT file to incorporate XML data into it.

Procedure Reference: Create an XML File

To create an XML file:

1. Choose **File→New** to display the **New Document** dialog box.
2. In the **Page Type** list box, select **XML** and click **Create.**
3. In the new XML file, type the required data within tags.

> In XML code, the main object is called a node. You need to expand a node to view the objects that it contains.

4. Save the file.

Procedure Reference: Integrate XML Data with XSLT Data

To integrate XML data with XSLT data:

1. Open an XSLT file.
2. Choose **Window→Bindings** to display the **BINDINGS** panel.
3. Click the **XML** link to display the **Locate XML Source** dialog box.
4. Specify the desired option.
    - Attach a file from the local hard drive.
        a. Select **Attach a local file on my computer or local area network.**
        b. Click **Browse** and navigate to the folder that contains the XML file.
        c. Select the XML file and click **OK.**
    - Attach a file from the Internet.
        a. Select **Attach a remote file on the Internet.**
        b. In the text box, type the URL of a file.
5. Click **OK** to integrate the XML file with the current XSLT file. The **BINDINGS** panel will display the schema of the XML.

Procedure Reference: Display XML Data on XSLT Pages

To display XML data on XSLT pages:

1. Open the XSLT file that has an XML document attached to it.

2. If necessary, create a table.

> In the XML file, the number of columns within a table should be equal to the number of attributes entered within a node.

3. Insert attributes on the web page.
   - Insert attributes using the **XPath Expression Builder (Dynamic Text)** dialog box.
     a. Position the mouse pointer at the desired location.
     b. Display the **XPath Expression Builder (Dynamic Text)** dialog box.
        - Choose **Insert→XSLT Objects→Dynamic Text.**
        - Or, in the **INSERT** panel, from the drop-down list, select **XSLT** and click **Dynamic Text.**
     c. In the **Select node to display** list box, select an attribute for the XML file.

> When you select an attribute in the **Select node to display** list box, ensure that you select the attribute corresponding to the column heading.

     d. From the **Format** drop-down list, select a data type format.
     e. Click **OK.**
   - Or, from the **BINDINGS** panel, click and drag attributes to the web page.
4. Save the file.
5. Preview the file in Internet Explorer.

Procedure Reference: Repeat XML Elements in an XSLT File

To repeat XML elements in an XSLT file:

1. In the document window, select all the attributes.
2. Display the **XPath Expression Builder (Repeat Region)** dialog box.
   - Choose **Insert→XSLT Objects→Repeat Region.**
   - Or, in the **INSERT** panel, from the drop-down list, select **XSLT** and click **Repeat Region.**
3. In the **Select node to repeat over** list box, select the repeating region element.

> The repeating region element in the **XPath Expression Builder** dialog box has a small Plus Sign (+).

4. Click **OK.**
5. Save the file and preview it in a browser.

ACTIVITY 6-5
Displaying XML-Based Data

Data Files:

meetings.html, boardmeetings.xml

Before You Begin:

From the **FILES** panel, open the meetings.html file.

Scenario:

You have a schedule of the quarterly management meetings that are to take place in your company. You need to display this data on a web page. Since the schedule needs to be constantly updated, you feel that using XML data will help you easily update the page.

What You Do	How You Do It
1. Create an XSLT file from the HTML file.	a. Choose **File→Convert→XSLT 1.0**. b. Verify that the meetings.xsl file is created and is selected as the current document. c. Choose **Window→Bindings**. d. In the **BINDINGS** panel, click the **XML** link.

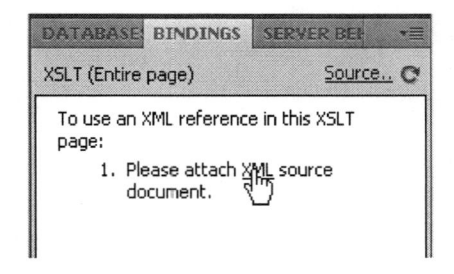

2.	Attach the XML data source to the XSLT file.	a.	In the **Locate XML Source** dialog box, verify that the **Attach a local file on my computer or local area network** option is selected and click **Browse**.
		b.	Select the **boardmeetings.xml** file and click **OK.**
		c.	In the **Locate XML Source** dialog box, click **OK** to attach the XML file to the XSLT document.
		d.	Verify that a schema for the XML file appears in the **BINDINGS** panel.
3.	Define a repeating region to display data.	a.	In the document window, in the second row of the table, click in the first cell.
		b.	In the tag selector, select **<tr>** to select the entire row.
		c.	Choose **Insert→XSLT Objects→Repeat Region** to display the **XPath Expression Builder (Repeat Region)** dialog box.
		d.	In the **Select node to repeat over** list box, select **meeting.**
		e.	Click **OK.**
4.	Insert XML data elements into the table.	a.	From the **BINDINGS** panel, click and drag **date** to the first cell of the second row of the table.
		b.	Similarly, add the dynamic text, "time" and "venue" in the second and third cells of the second row of the table.

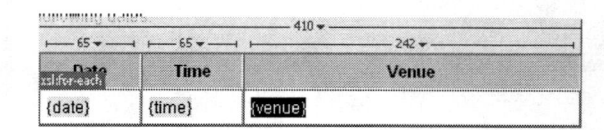

Date	Time	Venue
xsl:for-each {date}	{time}	{venue}

5. Preview the web page in a browser.
    a. Save the file.
    b. Preview the web page in Internet Explorer.
    c. Observe that the data from the XML file is displayed on the web page.
    d. Close the Internet Explorer window.
    e. Close all open files.

Lesson 6 Follow-up

In this lesson, you integrated external files with Dreamweaver. By integrating external files, you can update content on your web pages quickly with minimal effort.

1. **Which type of external files will you use on your web pages? Why?**

2. **Why would you integrate XML data to a web page?**

Follow-up

In this course, you used the advanced features of Dreamweaver CS4 to enhance websites. By using advanced techniques, you can make websites interactive and dynamic, and provide added functionality for site visitors.

1. **Which feature would you use to enhance the presentation of content on web pages?**

2. **Which Spry elements would you use on your web pages? How do you find them useful?**

3. **Which techniques would you use to display dynamic data on your web pages? Why?**

What's Next?

Adobe® Dreamweaver® CS4: Level 3 is the next course in this series. In this course, you will create dynamic, database-driven websites.

A | Working with Adobe Bridge and Adobe Device Central

Lesson Time: 1 hour(s), 5 minutes

Objectives:

In this lesson, you will work with Adobe® Bridge® and Adobe® Device Central® applications.

You will:

- Explore Adobe Bridge.
- Apply metadata and keywords to assets in Adobe Bridge.
- Work with stacks and filters in Adobe Bridge.
- Preview web pages in Device Central.

Introduction

You created websites using Dreamweaver. During the course of your work, you may have to organize the assets used on your website and preview the web pages as they would appear on mobile devices. In this lesson, you will work with Adobe Bridge and Adobe Device Central.

While working on a website, there may be times when you need to use other applications to perform tasks that will improve your workflow. Managing all the assets used on your website manually or previewing web pages on mobile devices will be tedious. Using specialized applications such as Adobe Bridge and Adobe Device Central will help you perform tasks with ease.

TOPIC A
Explore Adobe Bridge

You created web pages in Dreamweaver using assets from different applications. Now, you may need to access and manage assets created in Dreamweaver and other applications from a single location. In this topic, you will explore the Adobe Bridge environment.

Working with Adobe Bridge after familiarizing with its environment will help you manage the assets that are used to efficiently develop a web site. Exploring Adobe Bridge and understanding the components of its interface will enable you to use the application effectively.

Adobe Bridge

Adobe Bridge is a file browser that allows you to view, sort, and manage both Adobe and non-Adobe application files from within a central location. You can add and edit keywords and metadata; preview, rotate, and rank assets; and run batch commands. Adobe Bridge also includes a search feature that allows multiple search criteria. Bridge helps simplify work by enabling drag and drop of required assets into Adobe applications.

The Adobe Bridge Interface

The Adobe Bridge interface elements allow you to display and organize files.

Interface Component	*Description*
Menu bar	Contains the menu commands that enable you to view and edit elements in Adobe Bridge.
Panels	Contains a group of panels with a separate tab for each panel. Panels include **FOLDERS, FAVORITES, METADATA, KEYWORDS, FILTER, PREVIEW, INSPECTOR,** and **COLLECTIONS.**
Application bar	Comprises the navigation buttons, workspace presets, screen mode options, and a search text box.
Path bar	Contains options to create and delete folders and also sort files.
Thumbnail slider	Enables you to increase and decrease the magnification of the files in the **CONTENT** panel.
View buttons	Allows you to choose how the files are to be displayed.

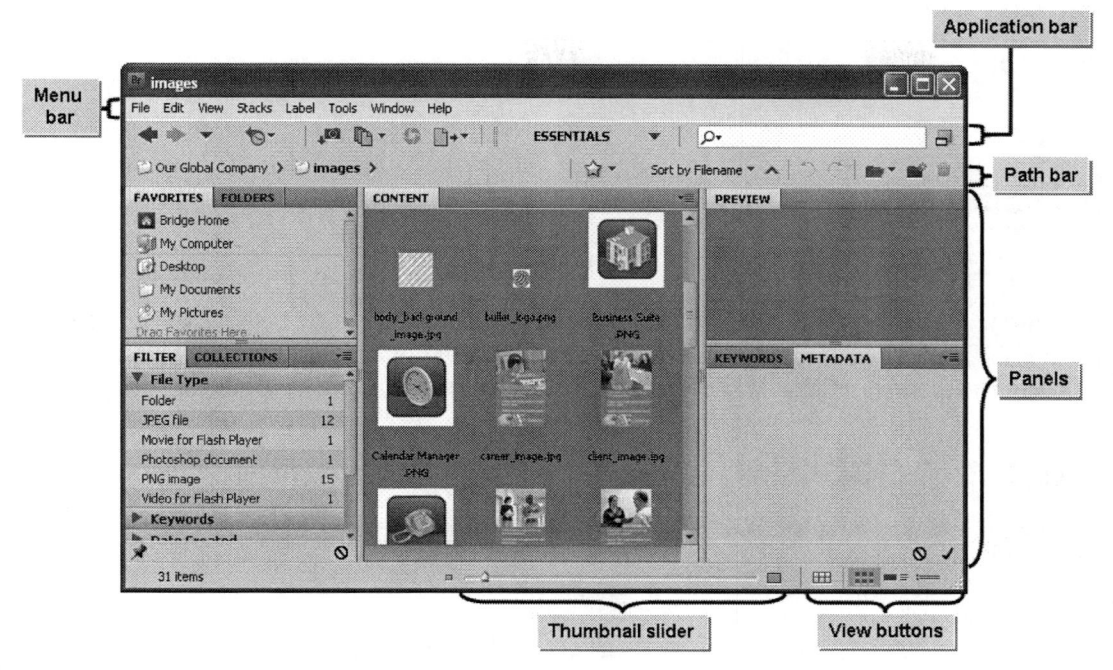

Figure A-1: Adobe Bridge helps you locate and categorize folders and files.

Adobe Bridge Workspaces

Adobe Bridge contains *workspace presets,* which are a collection of predefined workspaces that have panels placed in convenient locations to enable easy working. You can rearrange a workspace to best suit your creative workflow by moving, hiding, or displaying panels. You can save the customized setup as a workspace and activate it any time. You can also switch from one workspace to another, modify a workspace, or delete a customized workspace.

Panels in Adobe Bridge

Adobe Bridge comprises various panels that can be used to perform various tasks.

Panel	Description
CONTENT	Displays all the files in the selected folder.
FOLDERS	Displays all folders in a hierarchal structure.
FAVORITES	Contains the most frequently accessed folders and folders added as favorites.
METADATA	Enables you to add and clear metadata to assets.
KEYWORDS	Enables you to add keywords and sub-keywords to assets.
FILTER	Enables you to set criteria to control the display of files in the **CONTENT** panel.
PREVIEW	Displays the selected file and allows you to view it in detail.

Panel	Description
INSPECTOR	Displays information on the projects and assets managed using Version Cue®.
COLLECTIONS	Enables you to create a collection of files and smart collections that update automatically.

The Loupe Tool

The **Loupe** tool allows you to view the magnified portions of an image without actually increasing the image size. It provides a small preview on the image with the magnified display. The **Loupe** tool can be used only within the **PREVIEW** panel of Adobe Bridge.

Views in Adobe Bridge

Adobe Bridge offers several options for viewing files and folders.

View Option	Description
Slideshow	Enables you to view a slide show of all the files.
Review Mode	Displays window contents as a collection that can be scrolled like cards in a rotary card file.
Compact Mode	Reduces Bridge to a small window that can be floated like a panel.
As Thumbnails	Displays only a thumbnail of each file.
As Details	Displays the date and time of creation and modification of the files.
As List	Displays the files as a list.
Show Hidden Files	Displays hidden files such as cache files and provisionally removed Version Cue files.
Show Folders	Displays folders and files.
Show Items from Subfolders	Displays contents from within folders.

The Sort Options

Files can be sorted by criteria chosen from the **Sort Manually** drop-down list on the **Path** bar or using the **Sort** submenu from the **View** menu. You can sort the files by **Filename, File size, Date Created,** and **Date Modified,** or by properties such as **Dimensions, Resolution,** and **Color Profile.** You can also choose to sort files manually by dragging and placing them.

How to Explore Adobe Bridge

Procedure Reference: Explore Adobe Bridge

To explore Adobe Bridge:

1. Launch Adobe Bridge.
   - In Dreamweaver, choose **File→Browse in Bridge.**
   - Or, choose **Start→All Programs→Adobe Bridge CS4.**
2. On the **Path** bar, click an option.
   - Click the folder names to navigate to a folder.
   - Click the **Create a new folder** button to create a folder.
   - Click the **Open recent file** button and from the drop-down list, select a file.
   - Click **Delete item** to delete the selected file.
3. Choose a workspace.
   - Choose **Window→Workspace** and then choose a workspace.
   - Or, on the Application bar, click the drop-down arrow next to the existing workspaces and choose a workspace.
4. From the **View** menu, choose the view that you want the files to be displayed in.

Procedure Reference: Manage the Workspace

To manage the workspace:

1. If necessary, move a panel to a different location.
2. If necessary, resize the panel.
   a. Move the mouse pointer around the panel till it changes into a double-headed arrow.
   b. Click and drag the mouse pointer to resize the panel.
3. If necessary, hide the panel.
   - Right-click the panel and choose **Close [Panel Name].**
   - Or, choose **Window→[Panel Name].**
4. Create a workspace.
   - Choose **Window→Workspace→New Workspace** to display the **New Workspace** dialog box.
   - Or, on the Application bar, click the drop-down arrow beside the displayed workspace and select **New Workspace.**
5. In the **New Workspace** dialog box, specify options for the new workspace.
   - In the **Name** text box, type a name for the workspace.
   - If necessary, check the **Save Window Location as Part of Workspace** check box.
   - If necessary, check the **Save Sort Order as Part of Workspace** check box.
6. Click **Save** to save the workspace.
7. If necessary, choose **Window→Workspace** and then choose a saved workspace to display it.

8. If necessary, delete the workspace.
    a. Choose **Window→Workspace→Delete Workspace** to display the **Delete Workspace** dialog box.
    b. From the **Workspace** drop-down list, select a saved workspace.
    c. Click **Delete** to delete the workspace.
9. If necessary, reset the default workpace settings.
    - Choose **Window→Workspace→Reset Standard Workspaces.**
    - Or, on the Application bar, click the drop-down arrow next to the displayed workspace and select **Reset Standard Workspaces.**

ACTIVITY A-1
Exploring Adobe Bridge

Before You Begin:
The Dreamweaver application is open.

Scenario:
Having completed work on your website, you want to organize the files on the site systematically and group the assets together. Your co-worker suggests that Adobe Bridge is a great tool for managing files. But, before using it to manage your files, you decide to check out the application yourself.

What You Do	How You Do It
1. Explore the Bridge interface.	a. Choose **File→Browse in Bridge** to launch Adobe Bridge.
	b. In the **Adobe Bridge** message box, click **Yes.**
	c. On the Application bar, click **FILMSTRIP** to display the **CONTENT** panel as a horizontal strip at the bottom and the **PREVIEW** panel on top.
	d. Click the drop-down arrow beside the **OUTPUT** workspace, OUTPUT to view the workspaces available in Bridge.
	e. Select **Essentials** to revert to the default workspace.
	f. Select the **FOLDERS** tab.
	g. Navigate to the C:\084054Data\Working with Adobe Bridge and Adobe Device Central\Our Global Company folder and double-click the **images** folder.
	h. Observe that the **CONTENT** panel displays the content of the folder.
	i. Click the Business Suite.png image to display it in the **PREVIEW** panel.

2.	Create a new workspace.	a.	Right-click the **METADATA** panel tab and choose **Close Metadata** to close the panel.
		b.	Similarly, close the **KEYWORDS** panel.
		c.	Choose **Window→Workspace→New Workspace** to display the **New Workspace** dialog box.
		d.	In the **Name** text box, type *OGCWorkspace* and click **Save**.
		e.	Observe that the created workspace is displayed on the Application bar.
		f.	On the Application bar, click the workspace titles to switch between the workspaces.
		g.	On the Application bar, click **OGCWORKSPACE**.
3.	Add a folder to the favorites.	a.	In the **FOLDERS** panel, click **Working with Adobe Bridge and Adobe Device Central**.
		b.	In the **CONTENT** panel, click the **Our Global Company** folder to select it
		c.	Choose **File→Add to Favorites.**
		d.	Select the **FAVORITES** panel tab.
		e.	Observe that a folder named "Our Global Company" is displayed.
		f.	Click the **Our Global Company** folder to display its contents in the **CONTENT** panel.

TOPIC B

Apply Metadata and Keywords to Assets in Adobe Bridge

You explored the Adobe Bridge environment. You may need to search for files based on the file content or other specific details. In this topic, you will apply metadata and keywords to files.

When working with a large number of files, categorizing them will help locate specific files and group them. By applying metadata and keywords to files, you can manage and sort them efficiently.

Metadata

Definition:

Metadata is text that describes file properties such as creator, document type, and date created among others. In Adobe Bridge, metadata is stored using the eXtensible Metadata Platform, an XML functionality that enables you to share metadata with different Adobe applications. Metadata information can be used to search for and locate a file. You can add metadata to a file based on its type.

Example:

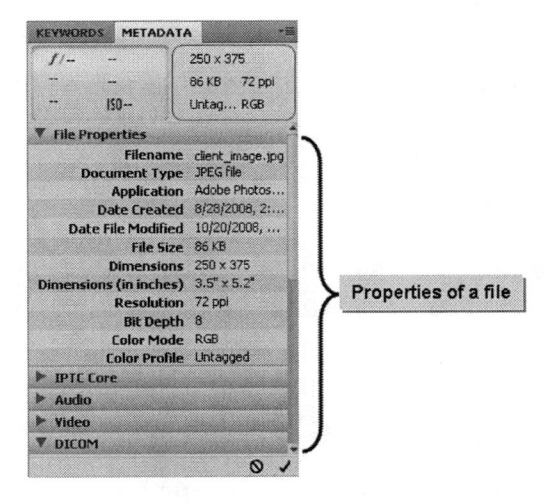

Figure A-2: The METADATA panel displaying the properties of a file.

Keywords

Definition:

A *Keyword* is a word that relates to a particular topic and can be used as a search term to identify files. The keywords are arranged in categories called keyword sets. In Adobe Bridge, you can define new keywords and create keyword sets from a group of keywords.

Example:

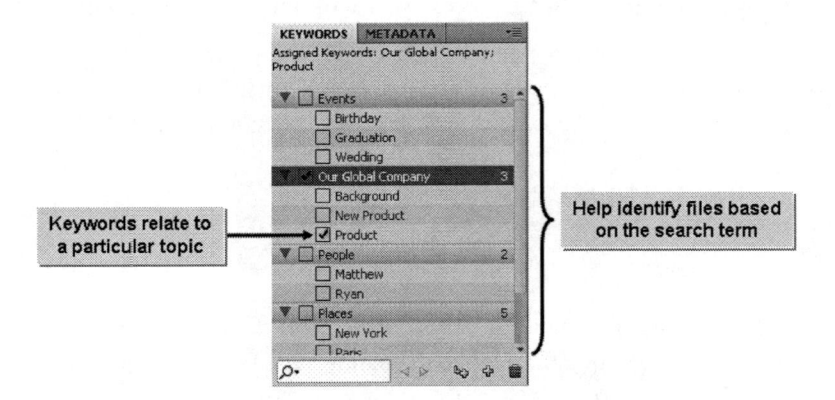

Figure A-3: The KEYWORDS panel displaying a list of keywords.

How to Apply Metadata and Keywords to Assets in Adobe Bridge

Procedure Reference: Apply Metadata to Assets in Adobe Bridge

To apply metadata to assets in Adobe Bridge:
1. Select a file.
2. Add metadata information.
   - Add metadata using the **File Info** dialog box.
     a. Choose **File→File Info** or right-click the file and choose **File Info**
     b. Select a tab and type the required content.
     c. Click **OK** to save the metadata for the file.
   - Or, add metadata using the **METADATA** panel.
     a. On the **METADATA** tab, click the **Edit** icon of the metadata item you want to add or change.
     b. Type the value of the metadata item.
     c. Click the **Apply** icon.

Procedure Reference: Apply Keywords to Assets in Adobe Bridge

To apply keywords to assets in Adobe Bridge:
1. Launch the Adobe Bridge application.
2. Select a file.
3. Select the **KEYWORDS** tab.

4. Define a new keyword.
   - At the bottom of the **KEYWORDS** panel, select an existing keyword, click the **New Keyword** button, and type the keyword.
   - Or, in the **KEYWORDS** panel, right-click any of the existing keywords, choose **New Keyword,** and type the keyword.
5. If necessary, create a sub-keyword.
   - At the bottom of the **KEYWORDS** panel, select an existing keyword, click the **New Sub Keyword** button, and type the keyword.
   - Or, right-click any of the existing keywords, choose **New Sub Keyword,** and type the keyword.
6. Check the check box for the new keyword or sub keyword to assign it to the file.

Procedure Reference: Perform a Search

To perform a search:
1. Choose **Edit→Find.**
2. In the **Find** dialog box, from the **Look in** drop-down list, select the source of the file.
3. In the **Criteria** section, specify the search criteria.
4. From the **Match** drop-down list, select an option.
5. Click **Find** to perform a search.

> After performing a metadata search, you can view the information about the file by choosing **File→File Info.**

ACTIVITY A-2
Applying Metadata and Keywords to Assets

Scenario:
The files you used for the design are organized in a separate folder. You want to use specific terms to easily locate files. In addition, you want to include your company's name as the creator of the design, so that you will be able to locate the file based on this information.

What You Do	How You Do It
1. Apply metadata to an image.	a. In the **CONTENT** panel, double-click the **images** folder.
	b. Right-click **Business Suite.PNG** and choose **File Info.**
	c. In the **Business Suite.PNG** dialog box, in the **Document Title** text box, click and type *Business Icon* and then press the **Tab** key.
	d. In the **Author** text box, type *OGC* and press the **Tab** key.
	e. In the **Author Title** text box, type *Our Global Company* and press the **Tab** key.
	f. In the **Description** text box, type *Product icon of OGC Business Suite*
	g. From the **Copyright Status** drop-down list, select **Copyrighted** and click **OK.**
	h. Choose **Window→Metadata Panel.**
	i. In the **METADATA** panel, in the **File Properties** section, scroll down and observe that the metadata entered is displayed.

Adobe® Dreamweaver® CS4: Level 2

2. Apply keywords to the images.

   a. Choose **Window→Keywords Panel.**

   b. Right-click the **Events** section and choose **New Keyword.**

   c. In the text box, type *OGC Website Data* and press **Enter.**

   d. Right-click the **OGC Website Data** keyword and choose **New Sub Keyword.**

   e. In the text box, type *Software* and press **Enter.**

   f. In the **CONTENT** panel, select all the images.

   g. In the **KEYWORDS** panel, check the **OGC Website Data** check box to apply the keyword.

   h. In the **CONTENT** panel, hold down **Ctrl,** and select all images with the blue and white background.

   i. In the **KEYWORDS** panel, check the **Software** check box to apply the keyword.

   j. In the **FILTER** panel, click **Keywords** to display the applied keywords.

Appendix A: Working with Adobe Bridge and Adobe Device Central

TOPIC C
Work with Stacks and Filters in Adobe Bridge

You applied metadata and keywords to files. You may want to organize files into logical groups so they can be easily located. In this topic, you will use stacks and filters to manage files.

When there are numerous files to manage, it is very difficult to locate them even in a centralized location. You can work meticulously if files can be logically organized into groups. Adobe Bridge provides options to easily locate and group files.

Stacks

Stacks is a feature that allows you to group files as a single thumbnail. You can collapse or expand a stack. When the stack is expanded, you can perform an action on the entire group at the same time. However, when the stack is collapsed with the topmost file selected, the action will be performed only to the file on top. When you group more than 10 images, the **Stacks** feature allows you to view the files in a sequence from the stack thumbnail.

Filters

Filters are criteria that can be set using the **FILTER** panel to control and manage the appearance of files in the **CONTENT** panel. Criteria are dynamically generated depending on the files that are displayed in the **CONTENT** panel. You can remove filters applied or even lock them to prevent them from getting cleared.

How to Work with Stacks and Filters in Adobe Bridge

Procedure Reference: Stack Files in Adobe Bridge

To stack files in Adobe Bridge:

1. In the **CONTENT** panel, select the files you want to stack.
2. Group the files as a stack.
   - Choose **Stacks→Group as Stack.**
   - Or, right-click the selected files and choose **Stack→Group as Stack.**
3. Open or expand the stack.
   - Choose **Stacks→Open Stack.**
   - Or, choose **Stacks→Expand All Stacks.**
4. If necessary, close or collapse a stack.
   - Choose **Stacks→Close Stack.**
   - Or, choose **Stacks→Collapse All Stacks.**

5. Preview files in the stack.
    a. If necessary, increase the magnification of the stack so that the slider is displayed when the mouse pointer is hovered over the stack.
    b. Click the play button to play the files as a sequence.
    c. Set the frame rate for previewing the files in the stack.
        - Choose **Stacks→Frame Rate,** and choose a frame rate.
        - Or, right-click the stack and choose **Stack→Frame Rate,** and choose a frame rate.
6. If necessary, choose **Stacks→Ungroup as Stack** to ungroup all the files.

Procedure Reference: Use Filters in Adobe Bridge

To use filters in Adobe Bridge:
1. Navigate to the folder where you want to search for the files.
2. In the **FILTER** panel, set the criteria based on which you want the files to be displayed. The **CONTENT** panel will display the relevant files.
3. If necessary, in the **FILTER** panel, click **Clear filter** to clear all the filters applied.
4. If necessary, click **Keep filter while browsing** to lock the filters applied.

Procedure Reference: Rate the Files in Adobe Bridge

To rate the files in Adobe Bridge:
1. Select the file or a group of files to be rated.
2. Rate the selected files.
    - From the **Label** menu, choose a rating.
    - Or, hold down **Ctrl** and press a number from one to five.

ACTIVITY A-3
Using Stacks and Filters to Organize Files

Scenario:
You used certain images from the support files for the creation of your web pages. These images share the same characteristics, and can be used in other projects also. You want to locate these images and organize them before sharing them with other members of the team.

What You Do	How You Do It
1. Set criteria to display relevant images.	a. If necessary, in the **FILTER** panel, expand the **File Type** criteria.
	b. Select **JPEG file.**
	c. In the **CONTENT** panel, observe that only files with the JPEG extension are displayed.
	d. Expand the **Orientation** criteria and select **Portrait.**
	e. Observe that the files in the **CONTENT** panel are updated to display only the images with **Portrait** orientation.
2. Group and rate all the relevant files.	a. In the **CONTENT** panel, select the files.
	b. Choose **Stacks→Group as Stacks.**
	c. Observe that the files are stacked and the number of files in the stack is displayed at the top-left corner.
	d. Choose **Label→**** to give the files a four star rating.
	e. Choose **Stacks→Expand All Stacks** to display all the files in the stack.
	f. Observe that the rating is applied to all the files in the stack.
	g. Close Adobe Bridge.

TOPIC D
Preview Web Pages in Device Central

You designed web pages and previewed them in browsers. Now, you need to check if web pages display as intended on mobile devices. In this topic, you will preview web pages using Device Central.

Displaying web content on mobile devices is essential as the number of users accessing the Internet through mobile devices increases everyday. Web pages that are created for access through computers may not display properly on mobile devices. Because the mobile device displays differ across models, it is almost impossible to determine if web pages will display correctly on all models. Adobe Device Central provides tools to preview web pages in a wide range of mobile device displays.

Adobe Device Central

Adobe Device Central is an application that is used to preview files created in Adobe applications such as Illustrator, Photoshop, Flash, and Dreamweaver on a range of mobile devices. It displays the skin of the selected device, and allows you to preview the file on a mobile device display. Device Central contains a library of sample device sets and also allows you to download device profiles of different mobile manufacturers from an online library.

Adobe Device Central Work Area

The Device Central work area consists of panels and tabs that allow you to access profiles of mobile devices and display detailed information about the selected device profile. The following table describes the components in the Adobe Device Central work area.

Component	Used To
DEVICE SETS panel	Create custom device sets by adding profiles of devices from the **LOCAL LIBRARY** and **ONLINE LIBRARY** panels. Device profiles can be selected from this panel to display the device on the **EMULATOR** tab.
LOCAL LIBRARY panel	Manage the profiles of mobile devices downloaded from the **ONLINE LIBRARY** panel. Device profiles can be selected from this panel to display the device on the **EMULATOR** tab.
ONLINE LIBRARY panel	Download device profiles from the library. Device profiles available online are grouped by manufacturer.
DEVICE PROFILES tab	Display the device profile(s) of the selected mobile device or a set of mobile devices.
EMULATOR tab	Preview the file on a selected mobile device.
CONTENT TYPE panel	Select the content type of the displayed file to test on the mobile device.
FILE INFO panel	View information about the file being previewed.

Component	Used To
KEY PAD panel	Simulate the appearance of the content on a mobile device when the keys on the device are pressed.
RENDERING panel	View the preview as it appears on a device that supports Opera's small screen rendering.

How to Preview Web Pages in Device Central

Procedure Reference: Preview a Web Page in Device Central

To preview a web page in Device Central:

1. Open a web page.
   - Open a web page in Device Central from Dreamweaver.
     a. In Dreamweaver, open a web page.
     b. Switch to Device Central.
        - Choose **File→Preview in Browser→Device Central.**
        - Or, on the **Document** toolbar, click the **Preview/Debug in browser** button and choose **Preview in Device Central.**
   - Open a web page using Device Central.
     a. Choose **Start→All Programs→Adobe Device Central CS4** to open the Adobe Device Central application.
     b. Choose **File→Open.**
     c. In the **Open** dialog box, navigate to a folder, select a file, and click **Open.**
2. In the **Adobe Device Central CS4** window, in the **DEVICE SETS** panel, double-click a predefined device set to display the skin of the selected device on the **EMULATOR** tab.
3. If necessary, in the **LOCAL LIBRARY** panel, expand a group and double-click a mobile device to preview the web page on the selected mobile device display screen.
4. If necessary, download a device profile.
   a. In the **ONLINE LIBRARY** panel, click **Connect.**
   b. Expand a group containing device profiles of a mobile device manufacturer.
   c. Double-click a mobile device from within the group to download a device profile and display the web page preview on the selected mobile device on the **EMULATOR** tab.
5. If necessary, at the bottom of the **EMULATOR** tab, use the rotation and magnification options to modify the preview.
6. Return to the Dreamweaver application.
   - Choose **File→Return to Dreamweaver.**
   - Or, choose **File→Quit.**
   - Or, close the **Adobe Device Central CS4** window.

ACTIVITY A-4
Previewing a Web Page in Device Central

Data Files:

index.html

Before You Begin:

Navigate to the C:\084054Data\Working with Adobe Bridge and Adobe Device Central\Our Global Company folder and open the index.html file.

Scenario:

You completed designing the Our Global Company website. Now, you want to ensure that the web pages display as intended when accessed through mobile devices.

What You Do	How You Do It
1. Preview the web page in Device Central.	a. On the **Document** toolbar, click the **Preview/Debug in browser** button and choose **Preview in Device Central.**
	b. On the **EMULATOR** tab, observe that the Home page is displayed on the default mobile device.
	c. In the **DEVICE SETS** panel, double-click **Flash Lite 2.0 32 240x320** to preview the web page in this device.
	d. On the **EMULATOR** tab, observe that the skin of the mobile device has changed and the Home page is displayed on a larger display.
	e. On the **EMULATOR** tab, on the skin of the mobile device, click the scroll down button to view more information on the page.

2.	Download a device profile from the online library.	a.	In the **ONLINE LIBRARY** panel, scroll down, and click the arrow to the left of "Nokia" to display the models of mobile devices from this manufacturer.
		b.	Scroll down and double-click **Nokia N96** to download the profile for this model.
		c.	On the **EMULATOR** tab, observe that the skin for the Nokia N96 model is displayed, and in the **LOCAL LIBRARY** panel, observe that the Nokia group is added.
3.	Browse the page in the mobile device.	a.	In the **RENDERING** panel, uncheck the **Small Screen Rendering** check box.
		b.	Observe that the web page is now displayed on the mobile device in its actual size.
		c.	On the **EMULATOR** tab, on the skin of the mobile device, click the scroll right button to preview the page on a device without small screen rendering.
		d.	Choose **File→Return to Dreamweaver** to switch to Dreamweaver.

B | New Features in Adobe Dreamweaver CS4

The table lists the new features pertaining to Adobe Dreamweaver CS4.

Feature	Adobe® Dreamweaver® CS4: Level 1	Adobe® Dreamweaver® CS4: Level 2	Adobe® Dreamweaver® CS4: Level 3
New User Interface (Application bar / New workspaces)	1-B & 1-C		
Integration with CS4 Suite - Photoshop Smart Objects		6-A	
Code Navigator	3-B		
Related Files		2-A	
Expanded Spry Tools		4-A & 4-B	
New Spry Form Validation Widgets		5-C	
CSS Best Practices (Property Inspector with CSS properties)	3-B onward		
HTML Data Sets		4-C	
Live View		4-C onward	
Subversion Integration			To be covered
Adobe AIR Authoring Support			To be covered
Code Hinting for Ajax and JavaScript Frameworks		1-A	

Lesson Labs

Due to classroom setup constraints, some labs cannot be keyed in sequence immediately following their associated lesson. Your instructor will tell you whether your labs can be practiced immediately following the lesson or whether they require separate setup from the main lesson content.

Adobe® Dreamweaver® CS4: Level 2

Lesson 1 Lab 1
Working with Code

Data Files:

info-center.html

Before You Begin:
1. Define the Citizens Info site using data from the C:\084054Data\Working in Code View\ Citizens Info folder.
2. Open the info-center.html file.

Scenario:

You are assigned the task of maintaining the Citizens Info website, which provides information to the citizens of the Chermont county. While reviewing the Information Center page, you noticed that a few modifications need to be made to the Community Facilities list. You also want to update the formatting style of table rows with a new style in all the pages of the site. As some of the team members will also be working on this file, you need to include description about specific code sections and information about the modifications required on the page.

1. Display the Information Center page in Code view, and add **Public Swimming Pools** as the first item in the Community Facilities list.

2. Indent the `<p>` tag in lines 181, 184, 188, and 191 to align each with the `<h2>` tag in the previous lines.

3. Collapse the `.tbody` and `.thead` CSS rules.

4. Add a CSS rule for the `<ul>` tag, assigning the value `square` to the `list-style-type` property.

5. Find **<tr>** tags with the class style tbody and replace the style with the **tabletext** style.

6. At the end of line 141, add the comment **This div container holds the main content of the page.**

7. Add a design note to the page, setting the **Status** as **needs attention,** with the **Name** as **Modifications required** and the **Value** set to *The Community Facilities and Major Service Providers of our Community sections need to be made more attractive.*

190 Lesson Labs

Adobe® Dreamweaver® CS4: Level 2

Lesson 2 Lab 1
Enhancing the Website Using Advanced CSS Styles

Data Files:

index.html, contact-info.html, background.gif, newlayout.html, banner.gif, rollover_up.gif, rollover_down.gif

Before You Begin:
1. Define the Citizens Info site using data from the C:\084054Data\Formatting with Advanced CSS Techniques\Citizens Info folder.
2. From the **FILES** panel, open the index.html page.

Scenario:

You have similar CSS rules defined on all the pages of the site. Therefore, you want to use a common set of rules for all the pages. You also want to properly organize information to enhance the appearance of the site and also provide a more attractive navigation interface.

---

1. From the Home page, export the **body, h1, h2, h3, h4, h5, h6, p** style along with the **h1** and **h2** styles to a new external style sheet named *citizen_styles.css* and save the style sheet in the root folder of the site.

2. On the Contact Us page, delete the **body, h1, h2, h3, h4, h5, h6, p** style, the **h1** style, and the **h2** style, and attach the citizen_styles.css file to the page.

3. In the citizen_styles.css style sheet, create a tag style for the `<body>` tag and add the following properties:
   - Background-image: images/background.gif
   - Background-repeat: repeat
   - Margin: 0px
   - Padding: 0px
   - Font-size: 12px
   - Color: #000

4. Open the newlayout.html file and attach the citizen_styles.css style sheet to it.

5. In the citizen_styles.css style sheet, create an ID style named *#banner* with the height set to 120 pixels and width set to 999 pixels, and in the newlayout.html file, insert a div container with **ID** set to *banner*, and insert the banner.gif image in the container.

6. In the citizen_styles.css style sheet, create an ID style named *#main* with the height set to 500 pixels, width set to 999 pixels, and background-color set to #FFF, and in the newlayout.html file, insert a div container containing the links with ID set to *main.*

7. In the citizen_styles.css style sheet, create an ID style named *#footer* with the height set to 40 pixels, width set to 999 pixels, and background-color set to #E38648, and in the newlayout.html file, insert a div container after the main container with ID set to *footer.*

8. In the main container, create a sub-container containing the links with ID as *links,* and another sub-container with ID as *text.*

9. In the citizen_styles.css style sheet, add an ID style for the links sub-container with the height set to 500 pixels, width set to 150 pixels, background color set to #EAEAEA, and float set to left, and add another ID style for the text sub-container with height set to 500 pixels, width set to 829 pixels, and float set to right.

10. Create an ID style named *#wrapper* with the following properties:
    - Margin: 0px auto
    - Width: 999px

11. In the newlayout.html file, create a div container with ID as *wrapper,* enclosing the entire content of the <body> tag within it.

12. Format the links as an unordered list.

13. In the citizen_styles.css style sheet, add a CSS rule to format the unordered list within the links container with the following properties:
    - Font-size: 12px
    - Margin: 0px
    - Padding: 0px
    - Width: 140px
    - List-style-type: none

14. Add a CSS rule to format the list items within the unordered list in the links container with the following properties:
    - Display: list-item
    - Height: 20px
    - Width: 140px
    - Line-height: 40px
    - Padding: 5px 0px 10px 0px
    - List-style-position: outside

15. Add a CSS rule to format the links in the links container in their normal state with the following properties:
    - Text-decoration: none
    - Background-image: images/rollover_up.gif
    - Background-repeat: no-repeat
    - Background-position: 0px 5px
    - Display: list-item
    - Width:120px
    - Padding: 5px 10px 0px 10px
    - Height: 35px
    - Color: #000

16. Add a CSS rule to format the links in the links container for the hover pseudo-class with the following properties:
    - Background-image: images/rollover_down.gif
    - Color: #FFF

Lesson 3 Lab 1

Creating AP Elements

Data Files:

info-center.html

Before You Begin:

Define the Citizens Info site using data from the C:\084054Data\Working with AP Elements\Citizens Info folder.

Scenario:

You want to display information about each service provider in a visually appealing way without obstructing other content on the page. You feel that allowing user interaction on the page to display this information will increase user interest.

1. Open the info-center.html web page.

2. Below the Major Service Providers of our Community heading, to the right of the Our Global Company sub-heading, insert an AP element named **OGC** and set the following properties:
   - Width: 225px
   - Height: 100px
   - Left: 360px
   - Top: 600px
   - Background-color: #EAEAEA
   - Padding: 5px 5px 5px 5px

3. Select the description for Our Global Company and move it into the **OGC** AP element.

4. Similarly, insert AP elements for the Everything for Coffee, Graser County Government, Chermont Medical Center, and Chermont University sub-headings named **Coffee, Graser, Medical,** and **University** respectively, and set the properties of all the AP elements similar to the properties of the **OGC** AP element, and move the information below each sub-heading into the corresponding AP element.

5. Hide all the AP elements on the page.

6. Apply the **Appear/Fade** effect to the text "Our Global Company" so that the **OGC** AP element appears when the mouse pointer is moved over the text and fades away when the mouse pointer is moved away from the text.

7. Similarly, apply the **Appear/Fade** effect for the onmouseover and onmouseout events for each sub-heading to display and hide the AP elements containing the respective information.

Lesson 4 Lab 1
Creating Interactive Elements Using Spry Elements

Data Files:

info-center.html, services.html, services.xml, universityinfo.html, catholic-churches.jpg, country-clubs.jpg, gym-and-aerobics-centers.jpg, jewish-synagogues.jpg, protestant-churches.jpg, public-golf-clubs.jpg, public-swimming-pools.jpg, public-tennis-courts.jpg, spa-and-beauty-centers.jpg

Before You Begin:

Define the Citizens Info site using data from the C:\084054Data\Working with Spry Elements\ Citizens Info folder.

Scenario:

As you review the pages of the Citizens Info website, you find that the information on the Information Center page can be presented in an organized manner so that it can be easily accessed and is also visually appealing. You also feel that presenting dynamic data on the web pages will help you present up-to-date content to site visitors.

1. In the info-center.html file, below the "Climate in Chermont" heading, insert a Spry tabbed panel, specify the tab names as *Avg. Winter Temp* and *Avg. Summer Temp.* For each tab, add the respective information from the table and then remove the table.

2. Assign *#FF8A00* as the background color for the selected tabs.

3. Below the "Community Facilities" heading, for the text "Public Swimming Pools", insert a Spry tooltip with the public-swimming-pools.jpg image and information on "Public Swimming Pools" from the tooltip.txt file.

4. Add tooltips for each facility below the "Community Facilities" heading, with corresponding images from the images folder and information from the tooltip.txt file.

5. For each tooltip, check the **Follow mouse** and **Hide on mouse out** check boxes. In the **Show delay** and **Hide delay** text boxes, type *100,* and in the **Effect** section, select **Blind**.

6. Modify the following properties in the CSS rule for the tooltips:
   - Background-color: #999
   - Border: thin solid #000
   - Font-family: Arial, Helvetica, sans-serif
   - Font-size: 10px
   - Padding: 10px
   - Width: 105px
   - Color: #FFF

7. Open the services.html file, and define a Spry XML data set named *dsServices,* using data from the services.xml file.

8. Enclose the table in a Spry region, and insert the **name, phone, workingdays,** and **hours** data elements from the **BINDINGS** panel into the respective rows in the table.

9. Enclose the table in a Spry repeating region and preview the file in Live view.

10. In the "Major Service Providers of our Community" heading, below the text "Chermont University", insert an HTML data set named *dsUniversity* to display the **universityinfo** table data available in the universityinfo.html file using the master/detail layout.

11. In the HTML data set inserted, in the detail container, add the labels *Dean, Undergraduates Enrolled,* and *Graduates Enrolled* for the respective data elements.

Lesson 5 Lab 1

Creating a Form

Data Files:

requestform.html

Before You Begin:

Define the Citizens Info site using data from the C:\084054Data\Creating a Form\Citizens Info folder.

Scenario:

You want to enroll volunteers for community activities in Chermont county. You want the community members to be able to register for voluntary service to the community.

1. In the requestform.html file, insert a form tag and move the table into the form.

2. Specify the form name as **RequestForm** and set the form properties to send the form data to info@citizensinfo.org on submitting the form.

3. In the "Name" row, insert a text field named **Name.**

4. In the "Phone" row, insert a text field named **Phone.**

5. In the "Email" row, insert a Spry Validation Text Field widget named **Email** and specify the type as **Email Address.**

6. In the "Confirm Email" row, insert a Spry Validation Confirm widget named **ConfirmEmail** and set its property to validate against the data specified in the "Email" field.

7. In the "Gender" row, insert a Spry Validation Radio Group widget named **Gender** and specify the labels as **Male** and **Female** with the values **male** and **female,** respectively.

8. In the "Which division would you like to volunteer for" row, insert a Checkbox Group element named **Division** with check boxes labelled **Parks, Recreation, Golf,** and **Zoo,** with the values **parks, recreation, golf,** and **zoo,** respectively.

9. In the "Please let us know a little more about you" row, insert a text area named **AboutYou.**

10. In the last row of the table, insert a button named **Submit** to submit the form.

11. Apply the **Validate Form** behavior to the form to ensure that users fill in the "Name" and "Phone" fields and validate that only numbers are entered in the "Phone" field.

12. Save the file and test the form by filling and submitting it.

Adobe® Dreamweaver® CS4: Level 2

Lesson 6 Lab 1

Integrating External Files

Data Files:

index.html, communities.psd, banner.swf, coffee.html, coffee.flv, newsroom.html, events.xml

Before You Begin:

Define the Citizens Info site using data from the C:\084054Data\Integrating External Files with Dreamweaver\Citizens Info folder.

Scenario:

You need to enhance the appearance of the community image on the Home page and ensure that it can be easily updated whenever it is modified. You want to enhance the overall look and feel of the site by using an animated banner on the Home page and a video on the Coffee.html page to complement the content. In addition to this, you need to add more news stories on the Newsroom page, which can be updated often.

1. In the index.html file, replace the image on the right with the communities.psd image in the images folder, saving the image in PNG format as *communities.png* in the images folder to create a Photshop smart object.

2. From the images folder, open the communities.psd image in Adobe Photoshop, turn on the visibility of the Enhanced layer, save the file, and update the Photoshop smart object on the Home page in Dreamweaver.

3. Replace the header image with the banner.swf Flash movie available in the images folder.

4. In the coffee.html file, below the heading "About Everything For Coffee", insert the coffee.flv Flash video as a progressive download video using the **Clear Skin 2** playback control, with the width set to *240* pixels and height adjusted proportionally.

5. Convert the newsroom.html file to an XSLT file.

6. Attach the events.xml file as an XML source to the XSLT file.

7. In the newsroom.xsl file, below the heading "Other News", in the table, insert the **eventhead** and **description** elements from the **BINDINGS** panel, in the first two rows of the table.

8. Enclose the table that contains the dynamic elements in an XSLT Repeat Region and select the **event** node as the repeating element.

198 *Lesson Labs*

9. Apply bold formatting to the **eventhead** dynamic element and italicize the **description** dynamic element.

10. Save the newsroom.xsl file and preview it in a browser.

Solutions

Glossary

Adobe Bridge
A file browser that allows you to view, sort, and manage both Adobe and non-Adobe application files.

Adobe Device Central
An application that is used to preview files on a range of mobile devices.

AP element
(Absolutely Positioned element) A block-level HTML element that is described by an absolute position and exact dimensions.

behavior
A combination of an event and an action that is triggered by the event.

Behaviors tab
Used to create and add new behaviors or alter certain parameters of behaviors that were created earlier.

code hints
A feature that lists the available tags or attributes that can be inserted into code.

coding context menu
Lists the most frequently used coding tools.

Coding toolbar
Contains options that help perform different coding operations.

comment
A nonexecutable statement that describes code.

CSS layout block
An HTML element that is represented as a rectangular box and used to position content on a web page.

CSS Layout Box model
A visual aid that displays the box model of the currently selected CSS layout block.

design notes
Notes associated with a web page.

filters
Criteria that can be set to control and manage the appearance of files in the CONTENT panel.

Find and Replace dialog box
Searches for text, tags, and attributes of tags, and replaces them with alternate values.

form element
Allows users to interact directly with a form and record their inputs.

form validation
The task of checking whether the user has entered the required data in the form and whether the data entered is valid.

form
An HTML element that gathers data from users and submits it to a server for processing.

ID styles
CSS styles applied to a single instance of an element on a web page.

Inheritance
The process by which CSS properties applied to an element are also applied to other element nested within it.

keywords
Words that relate to a particular topic and that which can be used as a search term to identify files.

Live view
A view that enables you to view your web page in Dreamweaver as it would appear in a browser.

metadata
Text that describes a file using keywords and other file properties such as the creator of the document, document type, and date created.

regular expressions
Patterns that help match combinations of characters in text.

RSS
An XML-based format that allows you to publish dynamic content on a website.

smart object
A linked image that is an instance of the original image used on a web page.

Specificity
The method of determining which rules apply to an element based on identifying which selectors are more specific than others.

Spry form validation widgets
Spry widgets that are form elements with support to validate user inputs.

Spry HTML data set
Used to display data available as HTML tables or other structured HTML elements.

Spry user interface widget
An element provided by Dreamweaver that displays data and enables user interaction on a web page.

Spry Validation Checkbox
A check box or a group of check boxes that validates whether the user has made the required number of selections.

Spry Validation Confirm
A text field that validates the user's input to match another field in the form.

Spry Validation Password
A password text field that validates the user's input for specified password criteria.

Spry Validation Radio Group
A group of radio buttons that checks whether the user has selected at least one option.

Spry Validation Select
A drop-down list that checks whether or not the user's selection is valid.

Spry Validation Text Field
A text field that validates user input for a specific type, format, and value.

Spry Validation Textarea
A text area that validates user input for the number of characters.

Spry XML data set
A tool provided by Dreamweaver to display XML data on a web page.

stacking order
A property of AP elements that determines the order in which AP elements on a web page appear in the browser.

Stacks
A feature that enables you to group files.

workspace presets
Predefined workspaces that have panels placed in convenient locations to enable easy working.

XML
A markup language for documents that contains structured information.

XSL
A family of languages for defining data and making it presentable on a web page.

Index

A
Adobe Bridge, 168
Adobe Device Central, 183
Adobe® Photoshop®, 144
advanced CSS selectors, 29
AP element, 62
Apply Comment, 3

B
Balance Braces, 3
behavior, 73
behavior effects, 76
behavior events, 75
Behaviors tab, 73

C
Code hints, 2
Coding context menu, 2
Coding toolbar, 3
Collapse Full Tag, 3
Collapse Selection, 3
comment, 19
CSS layout block, 39
CSS Layout Box model, 40
CSS Layout Outlines, 40

D
design notes, 18
dialog boxes
  Find and Replace, 11
  Image Preview, 144
  Input Tag Accessibility Attributes, 123
  Tag Chooser, 2
  Tag Editor, 2
DTD, 102

E
Expand All, 3

F
filters, 180
form, 116
form element, 121
form properties, 117
form validation, 131
Format Source Code, 4

H
Highlight Invalid Code, 3

I
ID styles, 39
Indent Code, 3
Inheritance, 30

K
keywords, 176

L
Line Numbers, 3
Live view, 103

M
measurement units, 41
metadata, 175
methods
  GET, 117
  POST, 117
Move or Convert CSS, 3

O

Open Documents, 3
Outdent Code, 4

P

panels
  AP ELEMENTS, 63
  BINDINGS, 102
  CODE INSPECTOR, 2
  COLLECTIONS, 170
  CONTENT, 169
  DEVICE SETS, 183
  FAVORITES, 169
  FILTER, 169, 180
  FOLDERS, 169
  INSPECTOR, 170
  KEYWORDS, 169
  LOCAL LIBRARY, 183
  METADATA, 169
  PREVIEW, 169
  REFERENCE, 3
  SEARCH, 12
  TAG INSPECTOR, 2
pseudo-class, 28
pseudo-element, 28

R

Recent Snippets, 3
regular expressions, 12
Remove Comment, 3
RSS, 158

S

Select Parent Tag, 3
Show Code Navigator, 3
smart object, 145
Specificity, 30
Spry form validation widgets, 131
Spry HTML data set, 102
Spry user interface widget, 86
Spry Validation Checkbox, 131
Spry Validation Confirm, 131
Spry Validation Password, 131
Spry Validation Radio Group, 131
Spry Validation Select, 131
Spry Validation Textarea, 131
Spry XML data set, 102
stacking order, 63
Stacks, 180
style overrides, 30
Syntax Error Alerts in Info Bar, 3

T

toolbars
  Related Files, 31

W

workspace presets, 169
Wrap Tag, 3

X

XML, 101
XPath, 158
XSL, 157
XSL-FO, 158
XSLT, 158

Z

z-index, 63